Bristol, Victoria Gazetteer, c.*1860*.

MONTPELIER
A BRISTOL SUBURB

The Old England, *a 19th-century painting by unknown artist.*

MONTPELIER
A BRISTOL SUBURB

Mary Wright

Phillimore

2004

Published by
PHILLIMORE & CO. LTD
Shopwyke Manor Barn, Chichester, West Sussex, England

ISBN 1 86077 284 6

Printed and bound in Great Britain by
CAMBRIDGE PRINTING

CONTENTS

For
Marianne and Alexander

LIST OF ILLUSTRATIONS

Frontispiece: The *Old England*

Preface and
Acknowledgements

Although there are references to Montpelier in most of the well known histories of Bristol, no study of the place itself has ever been published. Valuable research has been done by Alison Berkshire, Bridget Sudworth and the late Jo Harrison, and I am greatly indebted to their scholarly work, but none of it has reached the general public. In an attempt to rectify this I have brought together all the evidence I have found to explain the origin, rise and development of Montpelier and sought to interpret it against the general historical background.

The book starts by describing the wider area of Ashley, a rural part of the county of Gloucester, from which Montpelier emerges in the 18th century as a place with its own distinctive identity. It goes on to trace its evolution from an exclusive Georgian suburb, through a period of intensive development in the 19th century, to Montpelier's present status as an inner city area of Bristol.

I would like to record my thanks to the following for use of illustrations and photographs in this book:

Jane Bradley, Central Reference library, 2, 3, 4, 17, 18, 21, 40, and endpapers; J.R. Cleverdon, 14; Michael Jenner, 28; Sheena Stoddard, City Museum and Art Gallery, for the frontispiece (ref. MA5679), 12 (ref. K198), 16 (ref. M3433;1296), 27 (ref. M3442); John Williams, Bristol Record Office, 7, 25, 55; John Winstone, Reece Winstone Archive, 59; Frances Wright, 58. I am especially grateful to Michael Tozer for his constant encouragement and generosity in allowing me to reproduce the following photographs from his collection: 19, 32, 33, 34, 36, 44, 45, 46. My thanks also to Lawrence Wright who provided all the other photographs in the book and to Martin Wright who helped compile the index.

I am greatly indebted to the Society of Merchant Venturers and to all those local residents who allowed me to study their property deeds.

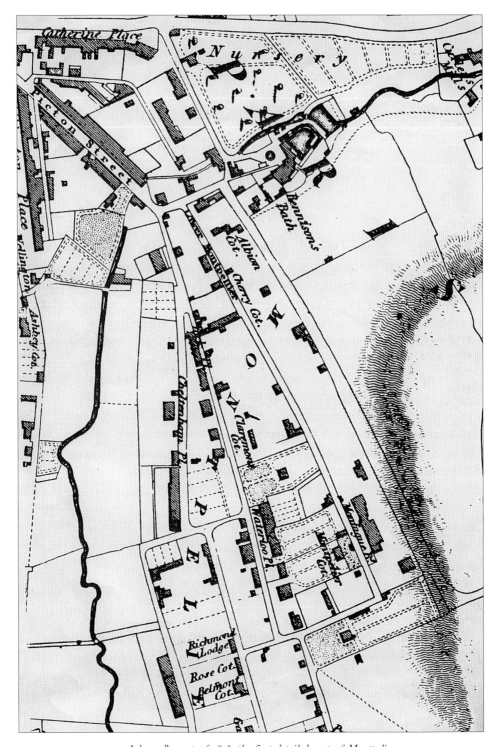

1 *Ashmead's map of 1828, the first detailed map of Montpelier.*

INTRODUCTION

The first question usually asked about Montpelier is why and when it was given its name. According to *The Place Names of Gloucestershire*, it was transferred from Montpellier, the spa town in the south of France famed as a health and pleasure resort.[1] Montpellier's assets were its elevated position, which used to be thought to guarantee pure air, its bathing facilities and its ancient medical school. It was well known to English travellers and a favourite destination for young aristocrats doing the Grand Tour with their tutors during the 17th and early 18th centuries. Until the French Revolution there was a flourishing colony of English residents in the resort. Montpellier's reputation led to its name being liberally applied, not only in Europe but in countries as diverse as Canada and South Africa, to any favoured location, but particularly to one that had fine views, wholesome air and clean water. Such places were often described as being 'fit to be the local Montpellier'.

Clues to the aptness of the naming of Bristol's Montpelier can be found in Matthew's *Complete Guide and Bristol Directory* published in 1794: 'There is a beautiful view of Bristol and the country from Montpelier which is situated not half a mile from Stokes Croft turnpike.' The guide goes on to describe Montpelier's other relevant feature:

> For those who are fond of bathing and swimming there are the spacious bath and dressing houses, pleasant gardens and good accommodations of Mr Rennison.

It seems that its topographical features combined with its reputation as a place for bathing and recreation were enough to merit the area being termed Bristol's Montpelier, albeit with only one 'l'. The date at which the name was first attached to the place is not known. As Matthew's guide proves, it was definitely in common use before 1794 and may well date from the opening of Rennison's Baths around 1747 (see Chapter 6). What is certain is that it predates by many years the indiscriminate appropriation of the name by the developers of the fashionable Regency streets, squares and terraces in Cheltenham, Harrogate, London and other towns. Further evidence of the local name's early use may be its spelling: one 'l' was more conventional in France before 1800. Other questions frequently asked about Montpelier concern its boundaries: where they are and when they were defined. At first the name described only the land and buildings scattered around the terraced hillside between Rennison's Baths and the top of what is now Cromwell Road. The earliest detailed map of the area drawn by Ashmead in 1828 (Fig.1) shows Montpelier Farm at the highest point and Lower Montpelier around the bottom of Richmond Road. As the neighbourhood became more built up the residents began to apply the name quite loosely to a much wider area. Then in the 1840s the growing suburb, which until that time had been in the outparish of St James and St Paul, was divided between the newly created parishes of St Andrew and St Barnabas. This radical change only added to the confusion about Montpelier's identity.

It was only when the railway was opened in 1874 that a recognisable physical boundary emerged. This was officially acknowledged in 1978 when city planning officers identified it as the northern limit of the Montpelier Conservation Area. The other boundaries were declared to be Cheltenham Road on the west, Ashley Road on the south and Ashley Hill on the east.

Although this book will be chiefly concerned with events that occurred within this area it will often stray outside it. Indeed, to discover the early history of Montpelier it is essential to do so.

One

THE ORIGINS OF MONTPELIER

1170-1579

The earliest documentary references to the area show that most of Montpelier was originally part of a large estate called Ashley. The name is a corruption of the Anglo-Saxon Asseley, which means ash tree glade or clearing.[1] This estate also included the land on which St Andrew's, Ashley Down and most of St Werburgh's now stand.

Ashley was in the county of Gloucester and formed part of Barton Regis, the farm estate of the king to whom all rents and revenues were paid. When, *c.*1109, Henry I created his illegitimate son Robert Earl of Gloucester he gave him the Ashley lands and part of their revenue. It was Robert who commissioned the building of the new Bristol Castle and shortly afterwards, *c.*1130, founded the Benedictine Priory of St James as a daughter house of the wealthy Tewkesbury Abbey.

Robert's son William, when he succeeded to the earldom, believed he could secure the future of the monks, and their prayers for his family's salvation, by adding to their land holdings. In 1170 he granted them his lands at Ashley which they were to hold as fully and securely as he himself had held them. The grant was confimed by Edward I in 1300 and by Edward IV in 1467.[2]

The monks' tenure was abruptly terminated at the Reformation. On 9 January 1540 the priory and all its lands were surrendered to the agents of Henry VIII. It was the last religious house in Bristol to be suppressed. In 1544 the king sold the priory buildings (apart from the nave of the church, which had become parochial in 1374) and its estates to Henry Brayne. He is usually described as a merchant tailor from London but, by birth, he was a Gloucestershire man, from an old Forest of Dean family.[3] After Henry Brayne's death, and that of his only son Robert, his property passed to his two daughters, Emilythys and Ann, with a jointure for Robert's childless widow, Goodith.[4] Both daughters had already made financially advantageous marriages, Emilythys to Sir Charles Somerset, son of the Earl of Worcester, and Ann to George

Winter, who had recently bought Dyrham Park. Since at that time the property of married women was vested in their husbands, it was Somerset and Winter who, in 1579, drew up a Deed of Partition which listed all the priory land and buildings and apportioned them between themselves.[5] It is this deed that provides the only written evidence of the nature of the area in the 16th century.

Ashley seems to have been almost entirely rural, an expanse of open and enclosed fields that were given over to pasture or arable crops, all farmed by tenants. The deed gives the name of each field and that of the current leaseholder. That does not necessarily make subsequent identification easy, for field names often changed when turned over to a new tenant or a different crop. Although no acreages are given, the largest landholding was likely to have been 'a great ground' called Further Ashley, probably what is now Ashley Down, described as being bounded by Glass Mill on the south, Horfield parish on the north and the land of 'the wild horse' on the east. West of this ground lay Higher Ashley, also known as Priorsfield, 'a great gated pasture' on which the roads of Upper Montpelier now stand.

The name Prior's Hill occurs three times in the deed, each time attached to a different location. One, which has retained its name, was part of the priory's Kingsdown lands; the others appear to have linked Lower Montpelier with the high ground of Ashley Hill. It may well be that the name was given to any rising land on the route from St James's Priory to Ashley.

The priory had considerable endowments in and around Bristol but the only one in the vicinity of Ashley, apart from Kingsdown, was Stokes Croft, pasture land which at that time contained only 'a little lodge and a garden plot in the entry'. At the upper end of Stokes Croft was a field which later became part of Montpelier. This was Apesherd, listed in the Partition Deed as 'a close of pasture with a little paddock in the tenure of John Hewardine or his assigns'. It is now the triangle of land that is bisected by Picton Street. It is the only part of present-day Montpelier that was not within the Ashley Estate. The estate's western boundary was, approximately, on the line of what is now Wellington Avenue.

The only agreement about the provenance of the name Apesherd (which has alternative spellings) is that it is ultimately of Old Norse origin.[6] There is demonstrably a long and continuous history of local usage. The name appears in a document of 1373 which describes the perambulation that was made to establish the boundaries of the new county of Bristol. These were marked by boundary stones, one of which was erected around the bottom of Ninetree Hill, 'opposite a certain path called Apesherd'.[7] The name was still extant in the early 19th century when the new houses in Picton Street and upper Ashley Road were described in deeds as being built on Apesherd.

In the division of the priory lands, Apesherd was allocated to Sir Charles Somerset yet some of its contiguous fields were granted to George Winter. In the absence of a neat geographical pattern of land distribution it is probably safe to assume that the objective of the division was to equalise the rental income between the two families.

The picture of the Ashley area that emerges from the 1579 document shows what a productive endowment it must have been for the monks, with its fertile land well wooded and watered by the streams that ran down both sides of Ashley Hill.[8] This patchwork of fields, gardens and orchards, with just a scattering of farmhouses, appears to have been a textbook example of an unspoilt 16th-century rural landscape. Evidence so far available indicates that it remained largely unchanged until at least the end of the 18th century. Any building that appeared in the interim was likely to have been a new barn or a farmhouse or, on rare occasions, a more substantial house built as a country retreat.

As always in the countryside, the arcadian idyll was underpinned by the real working lives of local people. Land ownership was concentrated in very few hands; everyone else had to make a living by leasing a few fields or, lower down the social scale, by agricultural labouring. In Ashley there was however the possibility of some alternative employment, although on a very small scale, at one of the watermills which, over time, became the nucleus of compact semi-industrial settlements in this rural setting.

Two

THE WATERMILLS

Two watermills were listed in the 1579 Deed, both on the east side of Ashley Hill. Some time later, probably during the next century, another two mills were built, this time on the west side of the hill. All the mills were fed by tributary streams of the River Frome. West of the hill four streams came down from Horfield and Westbury on Trym to converge around the bottom of Zetland Road. They produced a flow sufficient to power Cutler's Mill, which stood on the land between Station Road and Cheltenham Lane, and Terrett's Mill which was sited close to the present Montpelier Health Centre. Cutler's Mill Brook, as it was named, then turned eastward at the foot of Picton Street to run through meadows (now Shaftesbury Avenue) and eventually joined the Frome at Baptist Mills. On the east side of Ashley Hill streams that drained the valley between Horfield and Stapleton ran down to Boiling Wells in Ashley Vale. After merging with the Wells' overflow they went on to power Ashley Vale Mill, which stood in the garden of the present Mill House, on the corner of Boiling Well Lane. These streams, which became known as Boiling Wells' Brook, then continued on to Hooke's Mill, which stood at the foot of Ashley Hill, behind Ivy Church, to join Cutler's Mill Brook on its way to the River Frome. Although the existence and position of these mills is well documented it is impossible to establish their exact age or even, in some cases, their use.

Ashley Vale Mill

This appears to be the oldest of the four mills but it is also the least well documented. The earliest known mention of it is in a post-mortem inquisition of 1375 in which it is described as a water mill in Barton Regis. At that time it was known as Glaspelmuull (Glasspool Mill), from the primitive Welsh 'glass', meaning blue green, and 'pyll', a stream.[1] The name became shortened to Glass Mill, as in the 1579 Partition Deed where Matthew Smyth is shown to be

2 *Ashley Vale Mill, drawn in the late 19th century by S.J. Loxton.*

paying rent for 'Glase Mill'. Smyth, the heir to the Ashton Court Estate, was George Winter's cousin and, like him, a beneficiary of the break up of the monastic lands. During the 19th century it was usually referred to as Ashley Vale Mill. Its uses are not recorded, nor is the date when it ceased to be worked. On the 1882 Ordnance Survey map it is marked as a flour mill but that does not necessarily mean it was in use at that time. By the 1890s, when its rights to water were extinguished for a flood relief scheme, it was described in a survey as lying disused and unoccupied.

Hook/Hooke's[2] Mill (formerly Greene's or Grove Mill)

There is rather more information available about this mill. In 1548 Henry Brayne granted to his son Robert certain arable land and 'a water mill, formerly in the tenure of John Greene'. By 1579 the tenancy had descended to Thomas and William Greene. At some indeterminate time it was held by Walter Grove but the ownership remained with the Brayne family until one of their heirs, Sir Charles Gerrard, sold it and its land to Gabriel Sherman. By 1637 the mill had been acquired by Robert Hooke, a brewer, either as lessee or owner; at some point he bought the freehold but the date of the transfer is not recorded. St James's Outparish Census of 1637/8 lists Henry White and his wife as occupants of the mill, then the parish rate book for 1651 shows John Charles as the person responsible for paying the rate of 2d. per week.[3]

It was obviously a place of local importance. Millerd's trial map of 1670 marks the lane that became Ashley Road as 'the way to Hooke's Mill', and in Ogilby's 1675 strip map of Gloucestershire Hooke's Mill is one of the very few local places to be identified.

The fact that it was bought by a family of brewers bears out a subsequent claim that the water of the Boiling Wells was rich in sulphates and therefore particularly good for brewing ale.[4]

Hooke's Mill alehouse is mentioned in a newspaper advertisement of 1742,[5] and an account of the perambulation of the parish, known as 'beating the bounds', on Ascension Day 1751 reads: 'we come to a place called Hooke's Mill where the boys have cakes and ale, as customary'.[6]

In 1823 the mill was sold at auction for £3,020 to Robert Jones; it was a member of this family of flour millers, Henry Jones, who in 1845 invented self-raising flour. When it was next offered for sale, in 1870, it was described as a Powerful Water Mill working three pairs of stones, fed by the stream running from the Boiling Wells. In the 1890s the then owners, Messrs T.T. Chard, oil cake makers, no longer used the waterwheel but continued to take water from the millpond for their engines. Chards, who by 1919 had changed the name to Valenta Mill, remained there until 1927. They are the last recorded occupants.

Cutler's Mill

No reliable evidence has come to light to explain the origin of the name, nor is there any record of the uses to which the mill was put. The earliest reference to it comes in a deed of 1637 which verifies the sale by Sir George Winter and Dame Mary Winter of 'a tenement and mill, commonly called Cutlers Mill' which stood in a close of pasture named Oxleaze and the adjacent lands to Richard Aldworth and his son Robert.[7] The St James's Outparish Census of 1637/8 showed the mill and the land in the occupation of George Gulliford and ? Stevens (the christian name is indecipherable). According to the parish rate book, Mr Gulliford was still there in 1651 but after that date there is no mention of Cutler's Mill in any extant parish records or property deeds. The explanation seemed to lie in an extract from MS Bristol Calendars for 1664, quoted by Samuel Seyer: 'And Cutlers Mill was burned down to the ground on a Saturday night'.[8] However, since the mill is marked and named on Isaac

3   *The Mill Wheel, drawn in the late 19th century by S.J. Loxton.*

Taylor's, admittedly rather imprecise, map of 1777 it must be assumed, if the map is correct, that it was rebuilt, although there is still no information about its period of use. It is possible that one of the old routes to the mill still survives in Cheltenham Lane.

Paradoxically, although very little is known about the mill itself, its name has a long history of continuous use. This was because it was consistently attached to the nearby fields that were originally sold with the mill in 1637. They continued to be identified as the Cutler's Mill Estate until the late 19th century, when the last remnants were covered by the new suburb of St Andrew's. Ashmead's 1828 map shows a number of buildings on the site of the mill which were probably those painted by M.S. Williams in 1870. The artist, who lived directly opposite in Arlington Villas, Cheltenham Road, recorded the scene just before the ground was cleared for redevelopment.

Terrett's Mill

The earliest documentary evidence for the existence of this mill is an entry in the St James's outparish ratebook for 1708 which shows Thomas Melton paying a rate of 2s. 3d. (In the same year Hooke's Mill and land were assessed for 15s. 3d., an indication of the relative size and importance of the two sites.) Melton was at that time only renting the mill but in 1727 he bought it, and the surrounding land, from the owner, Joseph Jackson of Sneyd Park. The property deeds describe the site and the buildings that stood on it in 1727. It covered an area of one and a half acres and contained 'Two Messuages called Terrett's Mill, with a Smith's shop and water mill nearby', which had been built by Thomas Terrett. Cutler's Mill Brook ran along the west side of the mill and on its south side was a lane that led to Ashley. The new owner had 'the free liberty of passing through a lane that led from the premises to the great road from Bristol to Horfield'.[9] Joseph Jackson also owned the Cutler's Mill site and Melton bought from him part of a meadow in Oxleaze adjacent to the flood hatches. In doing so he became entitled to the materials belonging to 'the lately demolished Old House', the property of George Gulliford, the former occupant of Cutler's Mill. This seemingly unimportant detail may assume more significance when the later history of Terrett's Mill is related in Chapter 6.

No date is given for Thomas Terrett's building of the mill, nor for his tenancy of it. It may have been built after Cutler's Mill was destroyed in 1664, but that cannot be proved. The difficulty of the brook powering two mills lying so close together has been cited as a reason to suppose that Terrett's replaced Cutler's Mill. Against that it could be argued there was a reasonable land fall between them and that mills used to be erected wherever the force of water was sufficient to turn a wheel, even if the periods of use had to be limited. Thomas Melton built a house on the site, with a coach house, stable and carthouse attached and 'a Dyehouse next to the fishpond'. From this it seems that the mill was at that time being used for thread making, an inference supported by a deed of 1731 which records the sale of the property to a haberdasher who subsequently let it to a clothier. The next owner of Terrett's Mill was a baker, a Mr Vowles of Barrs Lane, St James's Barton. When he bought the site in 1744 he promptly built himself a grist mill and changed the dyehouse into a millhouse. Sometime later he converted his mill from grist to snuff grinding. In the middle of the 18th century the demand for snuff led to many corn mills being adapted to produce it. This resulted in a shortage of city bakers, of whom Mr Vowles was one, and caused the Grand Jury at Bristol's Quarter Sessions to deplore these conversions which might 'become very detrimental to the publick' and to endorse the Corporation's eviction of one of its tenants who had made the change.[10]

4 *The site of Cutler's Mill by M.S. Williams, 1870.*

In 1756 Mr Vowles sold most of the property to Jonathan Coram, an ironmonger, for £470. Part of the premises he sold was already let to Thomas Rennison, a threadmaker, at an annual rack rent of £16.[11] Rennison occupied the house built by Melton and rented the adjacent fishpond, dye and stamping houses and three linked gardens on the west side of the house. Mr Vowles, who had improved and developed the site during his ownership, retained for himself two small houses, some tenanted summerhouses and a stable.

By 1764 Jonathan Coram was bankrupt. At an auction of his property at the Exchange Coffee House on 4 October 1764, Thomas Rennison was the successful bidder with an offer of £300. The snuff mill continued to be rented by Jacob Eastbrook, a tobacconist and snuff maker, until 1802 when Thomas Richards, another tobacconist, replaced him.

Matthew's 1814 Street Directory includes a cornfactor, William Spencer, with an address at Rennison's Baths (the name later given to Terret's Mill) so by then the mill may have reverted to its earlier use. There is no evidence of any later tenancy although a mill was still on the site in 1824.

Three

THE LAND AND ITS OWNERS

The property transfers of a few wealthy families always play a pivotal role in the history of any area and that was very evidently so in Ashley. Indeed, the transfers of land and houses in and around the area were so inextricably linked to the fortunes, and misfortunes, of a number of such families that an account of one must, necessarily, include an account of the other.

The Somerset and Winter Families

After the dissolution of St James's Priory, Henry Brayne converted some of the monastic buildings into 'a capital mansion house'. When his sons-in-law divided the priory estates in 1579 they also divided this house; the Somersets took the eastern half and the Winters the western portion. Although there is now no trace of the mansion house, tangible reminders of these families remain nearby. A monument to the Somerset family is in the porch of St James's Church and a fireplace containing the Winter coat of arms is in Church House, the gabled house that adjoins the church. Sir Charles and Lady Emilythys Somerset had only one child, their daughter Elizabeth, who is shown with them in the monument. She married Sir Charles Radcliffe Gerrard and it was their son, also named Charles, who in the 17th century began to sell parts of the inherited lands.

The Winters were a much more prolific family, with branches in Lydney and Clapton-in-Gordano, whose names appear in many West Country property transactions. George and Ann Winter had three sons, the eldest of whom, John, served as Vice Admiral under Francis Drake on his voyage round the world. Since the Winters had helped finance the venture, John may have been sent to watch over the family's interests. His son, Sir George Winter, despite forcefully asserting his intention to keep all his estates 'in the name and blood of the Winters',[1] began to sell some of his Ashley lands before he died in 1638. His son, another John Winter, seems to have disposed of the rest, piecemeal, before his death in 1688.

The initial division and subsequent intermittent sale of parcels of these lands was to have lasting consequences for the Ashley area. The spread of ownership and the release of land for building purposes over a period of 200 years meant there was never any overall plan for development; the place just grew. It was the *ad hoc* nature of this growth that was largely responsible for the diversity in appearance and character that is particularly noticeable in Montpelier today. The land on which the suburb was built was conveyed in four major transactions at four different times, in each case to a different purchaser. But these seminally important land transfers also had a human dimension and some of the people involved in them were colourful and interesting characters, important figures in Bristol's history, whose eventful lives influenced their business dealings.

The transactions that determined the future development of Montpelier were the sale of Apesherd and that of three parcels of land in the Ashley Estate: the Cutler's Mill Estate; Higher Ashley, otherwise Priors Field; and Wheatstubs with its adjacent fields.

Apesherd

The perimeter of this land runs from the junction of Ashley Road and Cheltenham Road, along Ashley Road to Wellington Avenue, on through there to Bath Buildings until it reaches Cheltenham Road, then south back to the Ashley Road corner.

Apesherd was sold by Sir Charles Gerrard, grandson of Sir Charles Somerset, sometime during the 17th century but there is no record of when or to whom it was sold. A deed of 1744, in which Apesherd is described as a meadow or pasture land with a barn thereon, shows that three-quarters of the land was given as a marriage settlement to Mary Pittle and George Edwards, Gentleman, and that the other quarter remained in the ownership of John, Earl of Stafford.[2] In 1751 the Earl sold his portion to Sydenham Teast, a merchant and the first of a family of shipwrights who built and refitted ships at their Wapping Dock from 1750 to 1841. In 1766 Teast completed the purchase of the whole of Apesherd and at the same time bought Barnsleaze and Pyecroft, the fields at the foot of Ninetree Hill that are now part of Cotham.

Sydenham Teast died in 1773. The value of his estate, £30,000, entitled him to be included in a list of eminent local merchants 'who had but small beginings but died rich', although, it should be added, he was at the lower end of that scale.[3] His son, another Sydenham Teast, appeared to dissipate his inheritance quite rapidly. By 1796 he had incurred such heavy debts that his creditors insisted that he sell Apesherd. It was offered for sale at an auction at the Exchange Coffee House on 1 March 1800 but had to be withdrawn because it

5   *Memorial to Sir Charles Somerset, his wife Emilythys, née Brayne, and their only child, Elizabeth, in the porch of St James's Priory Church.*

did not reach its reserve price. It was bought immediately afterwards by Daniel Wait, a grocer and former mayor of Bristol, who paid £1,775 for the 9 acres, 2 roods and 11 perches which were divided into two closes. The new owner intended to secure a good return on his investment by building on the land. Within the next 20 years he and his successors would transform Apesherd from an agricultural smallholding into a fully developed surburban residential and shopping area.

The Cutler's Mill Estate

This estate extended from, and included, the north side of Bath Buildings, St Andrew's Road, and Fairfield Road over almost the whole of what is now St Andrew's.

The transaction in which Sir George and Dame Mary Winter sold Cutler's Mill and nearby fields to Richard and Robert Aldworth in 1637 effectively detached this land from the Ashley Estate. Although in some deeds it continued to be called 'Cutler's Mill, otherwise Ashley', it soon became known as the

Cutler's Mill Estate. Then, in the 19th century, it became in turn the Montpelier and the St Andrew's Estate.

The 1637 deed is very fragile and pieces of the parchment that contain vital place names have crumbled away. It is, however, still possible to glean some information about the estate's fields and boundaries. Oxleaze, where the mill stood, seems to have been one large field which bordered the highway from Bristol to Horfield. Other fields mentioned include Somerleaze, Stoball Leaze, Prior's Hill Field and Quarry Leaze; some of these were large enough to be divided into several closes. The estate was described as being bounded by Apesherd on the south; Ashley lands on the east; the lands of the manor of Horfield on the north, and the road from Bristol to Horfield on the west.

The new owners of this land belonged to one of the richest and most influential families in Bristol. Three generations of Aldworths had served as mayor, Richard was Warden of the Merchant Venturers, and both he and his eldest son Robert became MPs for the city.

When Robert married in 1652, part of the Cutler's Mill Estate was included in his marriage settlement. As was customary, the marriage was a union that cemented the bonds between two prosperous families. His bride was Dorothy Hooke, granddaughter of Humphrey Hooke, owner of the Kingsweston Estate, to whom the Aldworths were already connected through a marriage in an earlier generation.

Richard Aldworth died in 1655, leaving Robert all his 'lands at Ashley purchased of Sir George Winter'.[4] Out of the rents of these lands Robert was to pay his mother £40 a year and his sisters £100 a year during their mother's lifetime. Richard Aldworth's more personal bequests were: 'my White Mare; My Grey Long Coat, lined with fur, not once worn; My New Mourning Cloaks'. To his 'good friend Joseph Jackson' he left property and a gold ring. When Robert Aldworth died in 1676 he left his wife Dorothy, amongst other property, 'the little thatched house at Ashley'.[5]

In 1654 Dorothy Aldworth sold the freehold of the Cutler's Mill Estate to Joseph Jackson and his lawyer son, Nicholas; this family and their descendants continued to hold the land until the 19th century. The Jacksons obviously had sound instincts for investment for they also became the owners of Old Sneed Park. When Mary Jackson, described as a spinster of Sneyd Park, died in 1811 she left her property in trust for George Edward and James Thomas Martin, presumably because they were under age. In 1834 they sold a few plots of land in the Cutler's Mill Estate for building but retained the rest. This was sold much later and not fully developed until the end of the 19th century.

Higher Ashley/Priorsfield

This is the land to the south of the Cutler's Mill Estate on which nearly all the houses in the roads of Upper Montpelier were built. The exceptions were those on the Cutler's Mill land and a few houses near Ashley Hill which were built on land attached to Hooke's Mill. In the 1579 Deed it was described as a great enclosed pasture known both as Higher Ashley and Priorsfield, but on later estate maps only the latter name is used.

It belonged to the Somerset family, who sold it at some unrecorded date. The purchaser was probably an ancestor of John Bearpacker, a soapboiler who, according to property deeds, acquired the land by inheritance. He appears to have owned it by at least 1708 for the St James's ratebooks for that year show that he was assessed for 9s. 6½d. on his 'lands at Ashley'.

Property deeds give a more specific description of the land. It was taken out of three closes of 18 acres and one of five acres which was formerly called Chequer Ground, afterwards Hollister's Ashley. These names came from early lessees of the fields. Chequer Ground recalled Richard Rice (or Price) who kept the *Chequer Inn* in Wine Street and leased it, and other nearby fields, probably during the 17th century.[6] The Hollister association is not documented but the lessee may have been Dennis Hollister, owner of the Dominican priory buildings (now Quakers Friars) and, very briefly, MP for Bristol in 1653, or one of his family.

When John Bearpacker died in 1715 he left his property to his son, Sir George Bearpacker, who was married to Ann Dighton, a member of the wealthy Dighton family who owned land in Kingsdown. Sir George bequeathed his Ashley lands to his nephew, William Merrick, and from him they passed to George Bearpacker, a clothier of Wotton under Edge. His heir was his brother Edward, another soapboiler, and it was he who sold the first plots for development in 1792. Building then continued sporadically for almost a hundred years.

Wheatstubs, Longleaze and White Lyon Ground

These three fields stretched over 30 acres, from Apesherd eastwards towards Sussex Place. They are now the site of the houses in Ashley Road, the streets behind as far as Cheltenham Place and the covered water course of the Cutlers Mills Brook. Wheatstubs had at one time been leased by Richard Rice/Price of the *Chequer Inn* so it too was known as Chequer Ground. Wheatstubs was, however, the earlier name. Each of the fields had been sold in separate transactions during the 17th century by the Winter and Somerset families to Robert Hooke and his son Andrew, who went on to acquire the rest of the Ashley Estate that lay around Ashley Hill. The Hooke family held all these

6   *Elaborate canopied tomb of the Winter family in Dyrham church.*

lands until 1731. The new owners, the Bridges family, sold part of Wheatstubs
for building in 1791 but the rest remained in agricultural use. The next building
occurred around 1825 and continued at intervals over the next 70 years.

The Hooke Family

This family can be traced back to the 16th century. Their earliest recorded
ancestor was Elijah Hooke but nothing is known of him other than that he
fathered two sons, Robert, who purchased some of the above land, and
John. In 1600, when Robert was 15 years old, his father apprenticed him to
a Bristol brewer.[7] Robert and his wife Elizabeth had six children, the eldest
of whom, Andrew, served his brewing apprenticeship with his father. By
1674 he was wealthy enough to buy the Ashley Farm Estate from John
Winter. His eldest son, Robert, followed the family tradition by entering the
brewing trade. This practice casts an interesting sidelight on the relative value
placed on property and education during this period. In this and the previous
generation of the Hooke family it was the younger son who was sent to
Oxford University while the elder entered the family business at the age of
fifteen.

It seems that this eldest son may have predeceased his father for when Andrew Hooke died in 1687 he left his Ashley property and lands to his second son, Humphrey. For some unstated reason, but maybe because he had been educated for a profession, in 1688 Humphrey sold his estate to his younger brother, Joseph.[8] This was the year in which Joseph's first son, Andrew, was born and it is likely that the family would have high expectations of him. He had an impressive patrimony, mostly amassed by his grandfather, Andrew Hooke senior, who had bought land in the parishes of Horfield, Stapleton and St Philip and Jacob, but his largest single holding was in Ashley. It comprised 140 acres of farmland lying around, but mainly to the east of, Ashley Hill, and a substantial farmhouse and other buildings. He owned Hooke's Mill and its 15 acres of land at the foot of Ashley Hill and, to the west of the hill, the 30 acres of Wheatstubs and other grounds.

Andrew Hooke junior was to prove a maverick. He appears to have been totally unlike the grandfather after whom he was named. Firstly, he was not a brewer; when he was admitted as a burgess in 1713 he described himself as 'a gentleman'.[9] Secondly, he was to prove as adept at disposing of property as his grandfather had been at acquiring it. He was a man of diverse talents, an entrepreneur, historian and journalist. As a Justice of the Peace for Gloucestershire and a prime mover in the building of the Bristol Exchange, opened in 1743, he was a well respected figure. He wrote a history of Bristol entitled *Bristolia*, and founded and edited a local newspaper called the *Oracle*.

Despite, or maybe because of, his abundant energy and enterprise, Andrew Hooke overreached himself. In 1742 he was imprisoned in Newgate for debt. According to Latimer this descendant of a wealthy family was 'a man of literary attainments, but appears to have fallen from affluence to poverty through unfortunate speculations'.[10] While he was in prison his wife supported their family by opening a coffee house in Maudlin Street. After his release her husband gave tutorials at the coffee house, teaching geography and 'the use of globes'.[11]

Andrew Hooke's precarious financial situation was reflected in the property transactions recorded in the Ashley Estate deeds. By 1725 he was mortgaging parts of the estate to raise capital but he compounded his difficulties by defaulting on his repayments. Before long he was left with no alternative but to sell all his property, which he did in 1731.

Andrew Hooke's death in 1753 prompted the following notice in a local newspaper:

> Thursday last died Justice Hook, a Gentleman well beloved and respected. He had an annuity of £50 a year from the Corporation and Merchants' Hall of this city for his singular services in forming an excellent scheme for purchasing the lands for building the Exchange and establishing the markets of this city.[12]

This annuity ceased on his death and by 1757 his resourceful widow was reduced to addressing an appeal to 'the Humane and Compassionate'. Explaining that her husband had left her and their two daughters wholly unprovided for she related how, since then:

> his widow had supported herself and her family by printing the play bills for Jacob Wells Theatre in summer and keeping a Coffee House nearby. Now that the theatre is shut she is reduced to real want and asks for donations from the public.[13]

The outcome of her appeal is not recorded but Mary Hooke revived her printing business, removing it to Baldwin Street after the Theatre Royal opened in 1766. She died in 1774.

Meanwhile the Ashley estate had passed to a shrewd businessman, George Bridges, a Quaker and Distiller, who already owned extensive lands in Somerset and *The Seven Stars* in Redcliffe Street.[14] He completed the purchase of the Ashley lands in 1731 and in 1759 a survey plan was drawn to show exactly what he had bought from Andrew Hooke (see page 20). It is interesting to note that the link with the Brayne family had been retained, in Mr Brayne's Moor, next to Glass Mill.

The Bridges Family

George Bridges had not long to enjoy his new purchase. He died in 1733 leaving most of his estates to his wife Elizabeth. She subsequently married Alderman Jacob Elton and died in 1775, aged 80, having outlived two husbands and her only son, William Bridges. The Ashley property then passed to the two daughters of her marriage to George Bridges. Both daughters had married into prosperous Quaker families and, as in the Brayne family before them, it would be their husbands who would take control of their inheritance.

Mary Bridges' husband was Joseph Beck, the owner of Frenchay Manor; her sister Ann was married to William Champion, son of one of the founders of the Bristol Brass Wire Company. William became famous in his own right as the first person in Britain to make metallic zinc, thus laying the foundations of a very important industry. He invented the process when he was experimenting at his father's works at Baptist Mills but soon afterwards opened his own internationally renowned factory at Warmley. He then turned his inventive mind to solving the problems of Bristol's shipping trade: he built a dock at Rownham (later called Merchants' Dock) and devised a plan for a floating harbour. The cost of constructing the dock and the bitter business rivalries that were undermining his Warmley project eventually brought about his financial ruin. In 1769 he was declared bankrupt.

In anticipation of this he attempted to put his family's financial affairs in order. His wife Ann had died 20 years earlier leaving three children. In January 1769 William Champion assigned his interest in her inheritance to his eldest son, William Bridges Champion. Shortly afterwards that son died and his younger brother and heir, after a complicated legal action to break an entail on the Ashley lands, sold his portion of the estate to his uncle, Joseph Beck, for £7,500.

By 1776 Joseph and Mary Beck had become the sole owners of the Ashley Estate, which still included the 30 acres on the west side of Ashley Hill. After their deaths it was inherited by their only child, Elizabeth, who was married to Edward Ash, a raisin wine maker. When she died in 1823 she left her estate to be used for the benefit of her six children. Within two years most of the Ashley lands had been sold: the change from agricultural to residential use was under way.

Four

Early Houses

The only houses mentioned in the 1579 Partition Deed are some 'tenements' at Greene's (Hooke's) Mill. The earliest reference to a particular house occurs in a deed of 1630 which records that George Winter leased to George Pearce the pasture called Oxleaze 'on the road from Bristol to a town called Thornbury and the house built on part of it'.[1] There must have been more than one house on the Cutler's Mill land for another of the estate's deeds dated 1646 alludes to 'a close of land in Cutlers with houses thereon'.[2] Then there was the 'little thatched house at Ashley' mentioned in Robert Aldworth's will of 1670. Montpelier Farm, famous as the headquarters of Fairfax and Cromwell during the Second Siege of Bristol in 1645 (see Chapter 5), stood on Cutler's Mill land at the top of the present Cromwell Road. Obviously it too had been built in the early 17th century, or earlier, but there are no deeds to confirm a date. By the early part of the following century there was at least one other house on the estate, at Terrett's Mill (see Chapter 6).

No houses appear to have been built on Apesherd before the beginning of the 19th century. Building only started on Priorsfield in the 1790s but it is possible that one house on that land could have an earlier date. Number 95 York Road has been altered to such an extent that there are no external clues to its age. It is its position in relation to the linear development of the rest of York Road that raises the possibility it might have earlier origins. The fact that it is set back so far from the street may point to its having been a small farmhouse with a smallholding attached.

There were more, and better documented, houses on the rest of the Ashley lands. The earliest was probably a house, and barn, described in 1638 as having been 'latterly builded' on Sir George Winter's ground. This, and the 100 acres of land called 'Further Aishleys', were listed among Sir George's extensive property holdings at a post-mortem inquisition in 1638.[3] Given Sir George Winter's wealth it seems reasonable to assume that this was a substantial house.

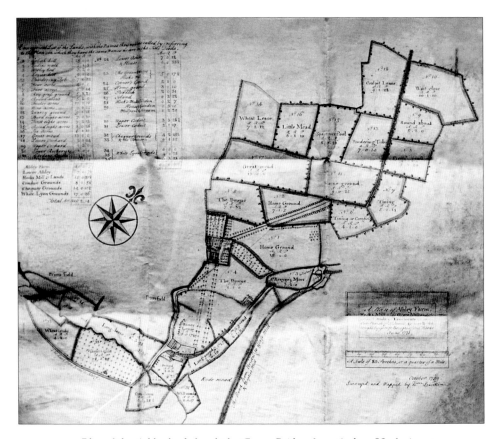

7   *Plan of the Ashley lands bought by George Bridges from Andrew Hooke in 1731.*

Speculation that it was the predecessor of Ashley Court cannot be confirmed, but neither can it be disproved.

Proof of the existence of the other early houses can be found in the deeds of the Ashley Estate and confirmation of their siting is provided in a plan of the estate drawn in 1759 to show buildings that were standing when the estate changed hands in 1731. Only one of the houses has survived but there is enough information about most of them to enable an accurate account to be given of the houses themselves and of some of their inhabitants.

Ashley Cottage, 77 Ashley Road
This is the only house shown on the 1731 plan that has survived. It had been thought to date from the 18th century until architectural investigation of the beams and ceiling plaster, carried out when the roof was repaired in 1970, revealed it to be of 17th-century origin. At the time it was built it would have been an isolated farmhouse at the extreme western end of Wheatstubs. The

only other pre-1731 buildings on that ground were a few tenements on the eastern periphery, near Sussex Place.

In 1666 Thomas Walter bequeathed the sum of £208 to St James's Church to be used to produce an income to buy bread each week for the poor of the parish. This money was invested in the land now occupied by Ashley Cottage, whose owner was to pay an annual rent charge of £10 8s. to the Feoffees of St James 'forever'.[4] Since that amount appears to have been paid by the owner or tenant of the cottage for the next 300 years it must have produced a copious amount of 'bread'.

A lease of 1796 contains a diagram of the layout of the cottage and a list of its fixtures. These included washstands, one mahogany, in the bedchambers; dressers; an ironing board; a kitchen crane with a smoak (sic) jack, and an oven and servants' bells in every room. Behind and around the cottage there were gardens and more than an acre of 'pleasure grounds'. The orchard contained 19 apple trees and an impressive collection of apricot, peach, plum, pear and cherry trees. There was also, among the outbuildings, the inevitable stable and loft.

Ashley Cottage remained part of the Ashley Estate until it was sold in 1825. Around this time it was tenanted by a series of professional or prosperous trades people. Deeds and parish records show a sugar refiner, a linendraper, a 'gentleman' and a Lieutenant Colonel of the East India Company at that address.

8   *Ashley Cottage, 77 Ashley Road, which was built in the 17th century.*

9   *Ashley Manor House with Hooke's Millhouse alongside in 1795. From the* Transactions of the
Bristol and Gloucestershire Archaeological Society, *1908.*

A later tenant, James Sangar, an upholsterer, bought the property in 1842 but
was declared bankrupt in 1849, whereupon his creditors sold it at auction for
£1,040.

By 1863 its name had been changed to Elm Villa, then in 1872 the cottage
and its land were again sold, this time for £1,500. The following year the
covenants that prevented building on the land were removed so that two houses
(Nos 19 and 20 Banner Road) could be built on the rear garden. In 1978 the
cottage was sold to Bristol City Council, who leased it to Avon County Council
for use as offices. It has now reverted to residential use.

Hooke's Mill Mansion House, later known as Ashley Manor House

This house lay at the foot of Ashley Hill, behind Ivy Church and alongside
Hooke's Mill. It was described, rather loosely, as being of the Tudor period
although there were some who believed it had earlier origins. Assertions made
by a few writers that it had been the guest house of St James's Priory, which
would place it before 1540, cannot be substantiated. Neither can the legend
that it was connected to the priory by a subterranean passage. The *Building News*
reported in 1907 that there was a passage which ran under Sussex Place but that
when a local resident had attempted to negotiate it he had been thwarted by a
fall of earth.[5]

A survey of the house before its demolition produced dates for some of its fixtures. A sundial under one of the gables bore the date 1656, one fireplace was inscribed 1659 and another 1669. These could, of course, have been later additions to the house so are inconclusive aids to dating the main structure. The fireplaces do, however, help identify the occupants of the Manor House during the second half of the 17th century for one bears the coat of arms of the Brewers' Company and the other that of the Hooke and Baugh families. The latter celebrated the uniting of two wealthy brewing families when, around 1640, Elizabeth Hooke, sister of Andrew Hooke who bought the Ashley Estate, married Robert Baugh. From architectural evidence it seems that this family enlarged and embellished the original house soon after they moved into it.

The house was occupied by the Hooke family or their tenants until 1731 when, along with the rest of the Ashley property, it was sold to George Bridges. He let it to tenants, one of whom, Father John Scudamore, was a Roman Catholic priest. The deeds do not give the dates of his tenancy but he seems to have been there before 1743. He is reported to have used an upper room in the house to celebrate the Mass. Since the first half of the 18th century was the period when rumours of imminent attempts to restore a Catholic Stuart to the throne were rife, the Penal Laws, which forbade the practice of the Catholic faith, were likely to have been rigorously enforced. So it seems strange that such tolerance was shown to the worshippers at Hooke's Mills.

The explanation lies in the need of the nearby Baptist Mills Brass Works for skilled and experienced workers. Such men could be found in the Low Countries but they and their families would only come to England if they were guaranteed the freedom to practise their Catholic religion. Since Baptist Mills was 'perhaps the most considerable brass house in Europe',[6] there were powerful economic reasons for granting this concession. Latimer states, without giving his source, that around 1710 'a few of the persecuted faith were

10 *The distinctive front door of the Manor House.*

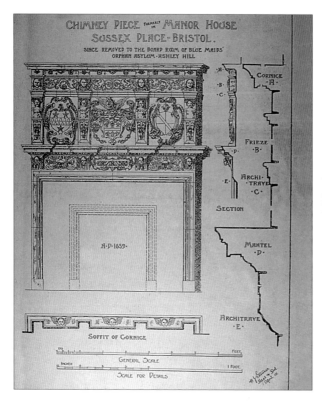

11 *A fireplace from Ashley Manor House now in the Red Lodge. Drawing from* The Building News, *5 July 1907.*

accustomed to assemble for worship in the upper room of a house at Hooke's Mills'.[7] If he is right then there was obviously a long established tradition of the authorities allowing a priest to say Mass in Ashley Manor House which may date from the opening of the Baptist Mills Brass Works in 1702.

In 1791 the Manor House was leased to the Magdalen Charity to be used as a refuge for 'deluded common women who wish to reform'. A chapel, now the much altered Ivy Church, was built for them and consecrated in 1792. The charity, which opened with 23 'penitents', had a very short life for, after the outbreak of war with France in 1793, subscriptions declined and it was forced to close the following year. The name survives in nearby Magdalen Place.

Edward Ash, the then owner of the Ashley Estate, was a member of the committee of a newly formed charity for orphan girls. He offered them a lease on the Manor House and on 12 January 1795 the Blue Maids Orphanage opened there with three children in residence. In 1825 the committee bought the freehold of the house but four years later, complaining of the unsalubriousness of the low-lying site, they moved to a purpose-built orphanage a little higher up Ashley Hill. They let the old house to a succession of tenants but failed to maintain the structure. Then, because they could neither sell it nor afford to repair it, in 1911 the committee agreed to demolish Ashley Manor House.

Some drawings of the exterior survive and in 1908 a local antiquarian carefully recorded the building.[8] By then some of the gables had been taken down but the picturesque huddle of chimney stacks remained, as did the windows with their oak mullions surmounted by drip stones. One particularly interesting feature was a distinctive ogee oak door, studded with huge nails, the main entrance. A visiting archaeologist described it as being identical to one in a house occupied by Cardinal Wolsey, who died in 1530. The house contained a wealth of early woodwork including a handsome carved staircase still in excellent condition, fine elaborate chimney pieces, and a ceiling with beautiful geometric strapwork which contained panels with cupid and pomegranate ornamentation.

Although it was judged to be the only surviving house of its kind in Bristol, substantially built and well worthy of complete repair, because of its location no one made the effort necessary to save it. It was stripped of its architectural features, some of which became showpieces in other houses. The ceilings are in Nailsea Court, a fireplace and a door are in Red Lodge and the oak panelling was re-erected in another, as yet unidentified, stately home. A local dealer offered £15 for the staircase but its ultimate destination is not recorded, neither is that of the fine ogee door. Another two fireplaces and three ancient panelled doors which were sold to the City Museum have disappeared.

Lower Ashley House

There is no such detailed account of this house but some pictorial evidence does survive. The plan of the Ashley Farm Estate shows it lying above Hooke's Mill, beside the Boiling Wells stream in what are now St Werburgh's allotment gardens. Evans, in his 'Outline of Bristol' published in 1824, describes it as 'the house in the valley, seated on the stream supplied by a spring called Boiling Well, and known as Lower Ashley House. The eastern approach to this mansion across the stream was by a gothic doorway and a bridge of stone.'

St James's parish ratebook for 1708 shows Andrew Pope, who was related to the Hooke family by marriage, as the ratepayer for Lower Ashley. He may have occupied the house at this time or, since the adjoining fields were also known by this name, the charge may have been levied on the land. Several sources agree that later that century the house became the country residence of Sir Michael Foster (1689-1763), Recorder of Bristol, Judge of the King's Bench and one of the founders of the Bristol Royal Infirmary.

Latimer states that when Sir Michael was elected Recorder in 1735 he 'took up his residence at Ashley'. Evans is more specific when he names Lower Ashley House as that residence. Richard Smith, senior surgeon at the Infirmary, in a letter to one of Foster's descendants, recounts a pertinent event that

12   *Lower Ashley House. Watercolour by F. Nicholson.*

occurred in June 1821. He had dined at the home of his friend, the historian Samuel Seyer, and afterwards the two men went for a stroll 'in the fields at the east end of Bristol'. They came to a house that had evidently seen better days which, Seyer assured his friend, had been the home of Sir Michael Foster. Smith, an enthusiastic admirer of Foster, then promised to have a drawing made of it. He later wrote, 'it was then inhabited by a sort of milkman. The whole property fell into the hands of "the Lunell Family" and as it was become rather an eyesore to "the Upper Ashley Court house" it was sold to a mason as materials for £24 and entirely demolished in 1827 so that probably the drawing is the only memorial of it'.[9] Richard Smith was wrong. A year or two before, J.B. Pyne, a Bristol-born artist who later became well known as a landscape painter, had made an etching of the house at the request of William Tyson FSA, proprietor of the *Bristol Mirror*. In addition, there are in the Bristol City Museum and Art Gallery another two watercolours of Lower Ashley House, one by Francis Nicholson RA (1753-1844) and the other by James Johnson (1803-34), painted in 1822. So this sadly neglected house has achieved some posthumous recognition.

Ashley Court

The Upper Ashley Court house whose view required the demolition of Lower Ashley House stood on Ashley Hill, on the site of the present Ashley Court Road. There are conflicting accounts of when, and by whom, this house was built. It has been attributed to Sir George Winter, to Andrew Hooke junior and to John Evans Lunell, but George Bridges's will describes it as 'the newly-erected dwelling house by me there lately built'. That statement gives the house a date between 1731, when Bridges bought the Ashley Estate, and his death, in 1733. It may be that Evans was right in asserting that the structure incorporated 'a house of previous erection' which, in 1824, 'still forms its west wing', although he was wrong in citing Andrew Hooke as its builder.[10] It is shown on the 1731 estate plan as 'courts and buildings', which lends some credence to that explanation.

George Bridges's widow continued to live at Ashley Court after her marriage to Jacob Elton and died there in 1775. The house was then let to the Reverend James New, the vicar of St Philip's Church, and he was followed by Isaac Riddle, a bacon merchant who was leasing some fields in the Ashley Farm Estate. In 1824 Samuel Lunell, whose brother John had just bought most of the Ashley lands, purchased Ashley Court and lived there until 1827. The next owner was Dr John Addington, who was described as 'a courtly and stately old gentleman',[11] an appearance rather at odds with his reputation as one of the most radical, avant garde, free thinkers of his generation and a fervent supporter of the French Revolution. He was the great uncle of the famous critic and essayist John Addington Symonds.

13   *This balustrade and the two stone pillars are all that survive of Ashley Court.*

After his death, and that of his wife in 1842, Ashley Court and some of its contents were sold by auction, the newspaper advertisement for which gave a very detailed, and effusive, description of the house:

> The Mansion, which is stone fronted, presents an imposing architectural appearance and, whilst placed on an easy eminence, sheltered from the many inconveniences frequently felt from the proximity of a road leading to a large city, embraces within its circle a panoramic view of scenery most luxuriant and picturesque.[12]

It was set in 4½ acres of lawn, shrubberies and garden and approached by a carriage drive from the road. The front lawn was bordered by 'a Grecian Balustrade' and at the rear were productive culinary gardens and a prolific orchard around which there was an 'inclosed private walk'. Another ten acres of land belonging to the house, which were 'admirably adapted for the erection of Villa Residences', were auctioned in three separate lots.

Ashley Court was bought by William Player, a mealman who was already farming in the nearby fields. He lived there until 1875. The following year the house was demolished or, as Arthur Salmon put it, 'the house was pulled down and its surrounding gardens and orchards outraged'.[13] St Werburgh's Rectory (now a hotel) and Ashley Court Villas were built on part of the site. Arthur Salmon, who had been so critical of the demolition, moved into one of those villas in the 1920s. All that now remains of the impressive residence are the Grecian balustrade and two stone pillars inscribed 'Ashley Court' and 'The Shrubbery'.

Ashley Farm and Ashley Grange

This house also stood on Ashley Hill, on a site above and adjoining Ashley Court, near the top of the present Chesterfield Road. It is not known when it was built but it must have been before 1674 for an indenture records that Andrew Hooke bought the Mansion House known as Ashley Farm from John Winter of Dyrham in that year. In an advertisement placed in 1742 it was described as 'a good Farmhouse':

> To be let at Lady Day next Ashley Farm consisting of 140 acres of meadow, arable and pasture land, well watered, wooded and having a good Farmhouse and other conveniences, within 1 mile of Bristol. Enquire of Jacob Elton in the County of Glos.[14]

During the next century the house was occupied by a succession of tenant farmers: Robert Francis, William and Isaac Riddle and Charles Jewell. In 1825 the latter was paying an annual rent of £300 for the farmhouse and lands.[15] During Jewell's tenancy the house may have been shared or sub-let for St Paul's baptismal records for 1814 show Thomas Young, yeoman, and his wife

14 *Ashley Grange, a Victorian house which was built on the site of Ashley Farmhouse. It was demolished in 1936.*

Jane at that address. By 1826 John Lunell had moved into Ashley Farm. Although it was a very substantial house, it does seem surprising that the major purchaser of the Ashley lands, who would presumably have had a choice of the properties available, should have preferred the old farmhouse to the more modern and stylish Ashley Court. He may have been thinking ahead for, at some time before 1846, John Lunell appears to have demolished Ashley Farm and built a new house on or near its site and a cottage in the garden. He changed the name, slightly, to Ashley Grange.

The new Victorian house with its coach house and stables, pleasant gardens and shrubberies was designed for gracious living. During the 19th century it had a number of owners, including W.G. Grace, who bought it around 1897 no doubt attracted by its proximity to the County Ground. During the 1920s it was adapted for use as a nursing home. It was demolished in 1936 for 60 houses to be built on its 5½-acre site. Although there is now no trace of the house, one of its garden walls may have survived: at the end of Ashley Park, off Chesterfield Road, there is a stretch of rubble wall which bears no relationship to the existing development; it may have been a perimeter wall of the Ashley Grange garden.

15   *Ashley Hill House was built before 1776. It survives although much altered.*

Ashley Barn

There are references in the Ashley Estate deeds to a barn built by Sir George Winter sometime before 1637. Its precise location is not known and the fact that Old Ashley Hill was called 'the road to Ashley Barn' is not particularly helpful. It seems reasonable to assume that it was close to Ashley Farm but it was not identified in contemporary maps.

By the 19th century it seems to have become a residence. In St Paul's baptismal register for 1817 Ann and Isaac Fowler, Gentleman, gave Ashley Barn as their address, as did Mary and John Perry, a farmer, in 1819. No account of the ownership of any property in Ashley in the early 19th century would be complete without the involvement of the ubiquitous Lunell family. In the estate rent book for 1823 Samuel Lunell is shown to be paying a rent of £60 a year for 'the messuage called Ashley Barn': this was just before he bought Ashley Court. After this date there are no further references to Ashley Barn so it seems likely that it was pulled down, maybe at the same time as Ashley Farm.

Ashley Hill House

Although this house is of later date than the others it does qualify for inclusion because it was part of the Ashley Estate in the 18th century. The date of its construction is not known but it was certainly there before 1776. A newspaper advertisement of 13 June in that year reads:

> Ashley Hill House. To be let with stable for 6 horses etc. Enquire : Jos Beck, 26 King street, Owners of the Ashley Estate.[16]

It has been suggested that around this time it was the home of John Bush, the mayor of Gloucester.[17]

The house, although greatly altered over the years, is still standing on Old Ashley Hill.

Five

THE FIRST CIVIL WAR
1642-1646

On 23 October 1642 the Royalist and Parliamentary forces fought the first major battle of the Civil War at Edgehill. On 4 December following Parliamentary soldiers entered Bristol. They garrisoned the city and held it until July 1643, when it was besieged and captured by the Royalists under the command of Prince Rupert, the King's nephew. The Royalists then occupied Bristol until September 1645.

Although at that time Bristol had a relatively small population of around 15,000, mostly living within the medieval walls, it was regarded as an important city. William Prynne, MP and Puritan pamphleteer, wrote, 'the whole kingdom looked upon Bristol as a place of the greatest consequence of any in England, next to London, as the metropolis, key, magazine of the West'.[1] Its strategic position as the main gateway to Wales and as a major seaport trading with Ireland, Europe and the New World made it of pivotal importance to both sides in this power struggle. A Royalist captain, Richard Atkyns, summed it up: 'when we were possessed of Bristol … I took the King's crown to be settled on his head again'.[2]

This connection must have been uppermost in the minds of the Royalist commanders in the summer of 1645 as the well-disciplined, well-paid New Model Parliamentary Army under General Fairfax advanced towards Bristol. After the crushing defeat of the King's forces at Naseby in June the military balance was tilting in Parliament's favour. In July its forces took Langport, stormed Bridgwater and secured the surrender of Bath. Then Sherborne Castle fell to them on 14 August. Bristol was now the only remaining Royalist stronghold in the West and the only seaport. If the King's men were to regain the initiative they had to hold the city.

Rupert was confident of doing so. He had a large garrison, strong fortifications and enough provisions for his soldiers and the townspeople to survive a six-month siege. Long before then, he believed, reinforcements from

Wales and the South West would reach the city. The Parliamentarians, equally aware of that probability, decided to concentrate all their efforts on taking Bristol as speedily as possible. On 23 August General Fairfax and Lt-General Cromwell set up their headquarters at Stoke House, Stapleton, where they held a council of war to review the state of the city's defences and to plan the details of their attack.

The old city was protected by its high stone medieval walls, strongly fortified castle and the rivers Avon and Frome. In addition there was an outer line of defence which consisted of earthworks, outside ditches, five-ft high ramparts and a line of bastioned forts to the north and west of the city. From the Water Fort (at the junction of Hotwells Road and Jacobs Wells Road) the line ran up to Brandon Hill Fort, then on to Royal Fort (a later house of that name now stands on its site), and through St Michael's Hill to Colston Fort on Kingsdown and Prior's Hill Fort near the top of Ninetree Hill. It then crossed Stokes Croft, obliquely, to continue to Lawford's Gate and the Avon.

Prior's Hill Fort was the largest and strongest of the forts. Its walls went up to a great height (a ladder of 30 rungs scarcely reached the top), it had two tiers of loopholes and was equipped with 13 cannon. Below it, near the bottom of Hillgrove Street, stood the well-fortified Stokes Croft sallyport. Realising that this fort was the key to the capture of Bristol, Fairfax decided that the main weight of his attack should be on the fort itself and the line from it to Lawford's Gate. With this in mind, he and Cromwell moved their headquarters to a small farmhouse on Ashley Hill (Montpelier Farmhouse at the top of the present Cromwell Road) and set up a detached bastion of cannon in the field behind. Its position, directly overlooking Prior's Hill Fort, was an excellent vantage point from which to conduct the attack. Cromwell wrote later, 'The general was extremely ill accommodated by reason of the littleness of the house, which he yet contented himself withal in regard to it lay so conveniently on any alarm.'[3]

Fairfax positioned his troops in readiness for the attack. Five regiments under Colonel Rainsborough were deployed in and around Montpelier. Rainsborough's own brigade was in Earlsmead (near Newfoundland Road), Colonel Birch's men lined up between Earlsmead and Ashley Road and behind them were Colonel Whalley's cavalry at the foot of Ashley Hill. Colonel Hammond's regiment covered the area from Ashley Road into Cheltenham Road, with Colonel Rich's cavalry in support on the site of Montpelier railway line.

At one o'clock on the morning of Wednesday 10 September 1645 the signal for the attack was given by the lighting of a bonfire of straw and faggots on Ashley Hill and the firing of four cannon in the field beside Montpelier

Farmhouse. 'Immediately the storm began around the city and was terrible to the beholders,' wrote Joshua Sprigg, Fairfax's chaplain.[4]

The Parliamentary army broke through the outer defences at Lawford's Gate and advanced to one of the medieval gates of the city. At the same time one of Colonel Rainsborough's regiments launched an attack on Prior's Hill Fort and the line down to the River Frome. Advancing under darkness, Rainsborough's men pressed doggedly up the hill under a hail of musket shot from the portholes and cannon fire from the ramparts of the fort. The walls were higher and the ditch deeper than they had calculated and their ladders reached only to the portholes. It took them two hours to gain possession of the parapet but that only resulted in a further two hours, fighting 'at push of pike'. The fort appeared to be impregnable and, as he later admitted, Rainsborough almost despaired of taking it. The breakthrough only came when Colonel Hammond, charging from Arley Hill, blasted open the Stokes Croft Gate with a petard and, after a sharp battle with the Royalist cavalry, drove the defenders back to St James Barton. This left the way clear for Colonel Rich's men to sweep up the Hillgrove (now Hillgrove Street) and link up with another infantry force that had broken through the Royalist lines on Kingsdown. Together they attacked the fort on its inner, weaker, side, scrambling through the portholes from where their ladders could reach the top of the towers. One of the first officers to reach the pinnacle seized the Royalist standard and tore it down. Outnumbered, the defenders retreated to the inner rooms below, hoping for quarter, but the Parliamentarians, inflamed by four hours of savage fighting and exasperated by the Royalists' stubbornness, were in no mood to grant it. They slaughtered nearly everyone in the fort.

Once their victory was confirmed, Fairfax and Cromwell, who had spent the night at their Montpelier Farmhouse headquarters, rode down to inspect the captured fort. While they were on the parapet a stray bullet fired from Bristol Castle grazed the wall within a foot of them. It would have been ironic, and maybe important for England's history, if Cromwell had been killed at this moment of triumph. Within hours Prince Rupert surrendered the city. The fighting was over in Bristol and within a few months the First Civil War had ended.

At his court martial Prince Rupert revealed that it was the loss of Prior's Hill Fort, 'an important place', that had influenced his decision to surrender and Cromwell admitted that the fort was 'the place of most difficulty'.[5] Cromwell wrote a long letter to the Speaker of the House of Commons describing in detail the capture of Bristol, and subsequent chroniclers have drawn on (and sometimes embellished) that account. All comment on the importance to the Parliamentary leaders of the strategically placed farmhouse at Montpelier. Writing in 1823 Seyer described the farmhouse as being 'situate on Ashley Hill, above Rennison's Bath', adjoined by a field where there was 'the trace of a redoubt, from which they cannonaded Prior's Hill Fort, distant almost half a mile'.[6] Another historian recorded that in around 1882 only two rooms of the farmhouse remained but that 'the remnants of the small lunette from which Fairfax battered the fort' could still be seen.[7] The farmhouse which had such momentous associations was demolished in 1886 and the field where the cannon had stood was levelled for house building. Although Lt-General Cromwell was of course junior to General Fairfax at the Second Siege of Bristol, his subsequent political importance was sufficient reason for him to take precedence over Fairfax when Cromwell Road was named more than two hundred years later.

Ashley Landowners

There is no means of knowing whether the people who worked in the fields of Ashley were loyal to the King or Parliament during the Civil War. They probably knew little and cared even less about the religious and constitutional issues that precipitated the conflict and only took sides when the fighting occurred close to home. This attitude may have been shared to a certain extent by many of those engaged in mercantile or domestic business in the city, who were likely to have been principally concerned about the disruption of trade or the heavy taxation levied to pay for the war. In contrast, from the beginning Ashley's three major landowners knew exactly where their loyalties lay: the Winters, Sir Charles Gerrard and the Aldworths were ideologically committed and overtly partisan in the conflict.

The large Winter family, dispersed around their estates in Gloucestershire and Somerset, were staunch Royalists. They played no part in the struggle for Bristol but were prominent in organising the defence of the areas around their country homes. In 1645 William Winter of Clapton was imprisoned by the Parliamentarians (despite his protestations that he had not taken up arms against them) solely on the grounds that he was a Winter and therefore must be a malignant.[8] The other members of the family seem to have retained or redeemed their estates after the war.

Sir Charles Gerrard also supported the King. He served in the Royalist army and was a member of the Council of War that tried, and acquitted, Prince Rupert of cowardice after he surrendered Bristol in 1645.

The Aldworths were steadfast Puritans and Parliamentarians. They were also resident Bristolians, actively engaged in the commercial and political life of the city. At this time Bristol was controlled by a small self-selecting group,

16   *Montpelier Farmhouse, headquarters of General Fairfax and Lt-Gen. Cromwell in September 1645, by T.R. Rowbotham, 1828.*

the members of the Common Council, who held in turn the offices of sheriff and mayor and who, with a few exceptions, belonged to the Society of Merchant Venturers. Their names appear with monotonous regularity in the legal documents of the day, conveying land and property to each other, witnessing each other's wills and securing and augmenting their family fortunes by intermarriage. Richard and Robert Aldworth were leading members of this oligarchy.

Richard Aldworth's career in public life fluctuated with the status of the Parliamentary party. When the Parliamentary troops occupied Bristol in 1642 he was mayor, but the following year, when the Royalists captured the city, he was expelled from the Common Council. According to his son John, at this time he was 'almost undone at Bristol most of his estate being seized on and possest by his enimies'.[9] He was reinstated after the Parliamentary army's victory in 1645 and elected MP for Bristol a year later.

His son Robert had a less fractured career. He was Town Clerk of Bristol for over 20 years and MP for the city in the three parliaments of the Commonwealth. When Richard Cromwell, Oliver's son and heir, visited Bristol in 1658 he was entertained at Robert Aldworth's mansion house in Broad Street. Despite his opposition to the restoration of the monarchy in 1660, and the King's explicit command that all supporters of the Parliamentary cause should be expelled from the Common Council, Robert Aldworth retained his seat. So too did Joseph Jackson, Robert's stepfather-in-law and fellow MP, who was described by Latimer as 'a zealous Parliamentarian and fractious Anabaptist'.[10] Those members of the Council who alleged that the two men only kept their seats through nepotism were probably right for both were related by marriage to the Royalist mayor and the mayor-elect.

This is only one example of the divergence of opinion and loyalties that must have occurred within many families during the Civil War and illustrates the speed (and no doubt relief) with which the wider questions of politics and religion were pushed aside and the old practical ties of kinship and business reaffirmed as soon as the conflict was settled.

Six

RENNISON'S BATHS

It was around the middle of the 18th century that Montpelier began to emerge as a place with its own identity, quite distinct from the rest of Ashley. This development was closely associated with, and may be largely attributable to, the enterprise of one man. The stories about the colourful life and exploits of Thomas Rennison may have grown in the telling but there seems no doubt that it was he who established Montpelier as a fashionable, if unconventional, place of pleasure, recreation and entertainment.

The main sources of information about Rennison are his own account of an incident that occurred in Montpelier, property deeds and contemporary newspaper advertisements. He was a threadmaker who came from Birmingham to Bristol with ambitions to set up his own factory. In 1747 he took a 17-year lease from a Mr Vowles on a house, part of a mill, a fishpond and a garden at Terrett's Mill at a rent of £16 per annum, with the right to use the water from the pond for two hours each day for working and beating his thread.

Within a few years Rennison fell into arrears with his rent. When he failed to meet his landlord's deadline for payment Mr Vowles sent in auctioneers to seize and sell Rennison's household goods. Later that day the landlord came with more men 'carrying lighted candles and beat down, in a violent manner, all before them'. We have only Rennison's own account of this incident, which he published in an open letter he addressed to 'the Worthy Citizens of Bristol, Encouragers of Art and Manufactories'.[1] After telling his story Rennison ends the letter with an appeal for money to help him re-establish his business. He cites the example of a Birmingham threadmaker who created employment for 1,000 people in his factory and predicts that, with financial backing, he could do likewise.

The style and audacity of this letter give some insight into the character of Thomas Rennison. The narrative is skilfully written and demonstrates his

37

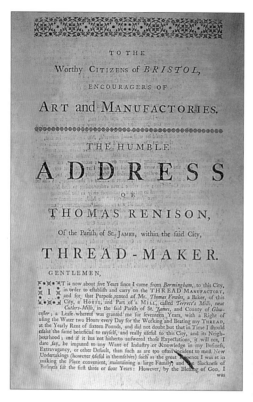

TO THE

Worthy CITIZENS of *BRISTOL*,

ENCOURAGERS OF

ART and MANUFACTORIES.

THE HUMBLE

A D D R E S S

OF

THOMAS RENISON,

Of the Parish of St. JAMES, within the said City,

THREAD-MAKER.

GENTLEMEN,

IT is now about five Years since I came from *Birmingham*, to this City, in order to establish and carry on the THREAD MANUFACTORY, and for, that Purpose rented of Mr. *Thomas Fowles*, a Baker, of this City, a HOUSE, and Part of a MILL, called *Terrett's Mills*, near *Cutlers-Mills*, in the said Parish of St. *James*, and County of *Gloucester*; a Lease whereof was granted me for seventeen Years, with a Right of using the Water two Hours every Day for the Working and Beating my THREAD, at the Yearly Rent of sixteen Pounds, and did not doubt but that in Time I should make the same beneficial to myself, and really useful to this City, and its Neighbourhood; and if it has not hitherto answered those Expectations, it will not, I dare say, be imputed to any Want of Industry or Knowledge in my Business, Extravagancy, or other Default, than such as are too often incident to most New Undertakings (however useful in themselves) such as the great Expence I was at in making the Place convenient, maintaining a large Family, and the Slackness of Business for the first three or four Years: However, by the Blessing of GOD, I
was

17 *Thomas Rennison's Address.*

undoubted flair for dramatic reconstruction. While it is of course partial and self-justifying, he is careful not to strain his readers' credulity too far. For example, his claim that his landlord's real motive was to repossess the property to relet it at a higher rent is perfectly plausible. On this evidence, although Rennison was certainly financially imprudent, he was also self-confident, resourceful and willing to take risks, particularly with other people's money. He could probably be described as an instinctive entrepreneur.

It is not known whether any worthy citizens responded to the appeal but Rennison never realised his grand plans for a thread factory on the Birmingham scale. However, he and his landlord must have resolved their dispute for an advertisement for the auction of the premises in 1764 shows that he was still the sitting tenant with a lease due to expire that year. It is ironic that it was Thomas Rennison who, at that auction, bought the property from which he had so very nearly been evicted.

> Auction: A handsome and commodious Dwelling-house called Territts Mills, in the Parish of Westbury-on-Trym, together with a Water Grist Mill, Stamping House, Outhouses and Garden. Also a large and commodious Cold Bath with a private one adjoining, much frequented and made use of for bathing, which baths alone bring in between £30 and £40 per annum.
>
> N.B. The Mill was lately used as a Snuff Mill and is now let at £4 per annum and the remainder of the premises (except the Baths) were let by Lease in the year 1707 to Mr Thomas Rennison, the present tenant, at £16 per annum for a term of 17 years which will expire on the 10th October next. The Baths have been made since the granting of such Lease.[2]

There are two errors in this auction notice: the placing of the premises in the Westbury-on-Trym parish when, as all records show, it was in the outparish of St James, and the date of the granting of Rennison's lease; 1707 must be a misprint for 1747.

This advertisement provides the first written evidence of Thomas Rennison's use of the site for purposes other than threadmaking when it describes the two baths, which were obviously popular and profitable. During his early tenancy Rennison must have observed swimmers coming out of the city in summer to bathe in the large natural pond at this quiet rural spot. He realised that there was the potential to develop this informal pastime into an organised commercial activity and to provide other recreational attractions for the visitors. His first step was to make a large circular swimming bath, 400 feet in circumference, to build dressing rooms around it and to charge for admission. He then added a smaller adjacent bath for ladies. A copper token in the City Museum, issued in 1764, bears on one side the inscription 'Rennison's Grand Pleasure Baths' and, on the reverse, 'Ladies Private Bath and Fountains' with the admission fee of 2d.

Encouraged by the success of this venture Rennison went on to provide more amenities on the site. He built a coffee house but soon converted it to a tavern which served 'Neat Wines, Rum, Brandy etc' and dinners 'drest on the shortest notice'. He laid out a bowling green and fitted up tea gardens 'in an elegant manner'. There on summer evenings he held concerts twice a week, admission 1s. to include tea or coffee. These attractions were laid out in enticing newspaper advertisements in which Rennison assured potential patrons that he would 'pay the utmost care and attention to render everything agreeable' to them.[3] But there is some evidence that he saw his enterprise as going beyond the provision of rather conventional activities for a paying public. He styled himself Governor of the Colony of Newfoundland and, paradoxically, named his tavern the *Old England*. Pursuing this theme of independence, he held an annual beanfeast at which, in a parody of Bristol's civic ceremonies, a mock mayor, sheriffs and other dignitaries were elected and the ruled became the rulers. According to Latimer, the none too abstemious revellers indulged in 'various high jinks',[4] which he leaves undefined. Part of the attraction for the participants in these licentious activities would be the certainty that they had nothing to fear from the civic authorities for the site was outside the city's boundaries and the jurisdiction of its magistrates.

There was a striking contrast between the wild subversive parties in the tavern and the decorous music concerts in the tea gardens. The two may have been no more than an expression of Thomas Rennison's dedication to providing the greatest pleasure for the greatest number or they may have reflected different facets of his own complex character. Whatever the explanation, it was this diversity that gave 18th-century Montpelier its distinctive character and its lasting reputation.

By the time of Thomas Rennison's death in 1792 the name Montpelier was firmly attached to the area. It seems highly likely that this, too, was indirectly due to him. While it is possible that the natural features of the local landscape, its terraced hillside and good viewpoint, may in themselves have been sufficient reason to liken it to the French spa town, it seems more than coincidence that the first recorded use of the name for this area occurred only after the opening of Rennison's Baths.

The absence of publicity for the Pleasure Gardens after his death reinforces the theory that it was he alone who was responsible for the ideas and organisation that underpinned their success. He was also responsible for the funding of the venture, however, and it is here that his central weakness is revealed. His entrepreneurial flair far outstripped his financial competence and the earlier dispute over his non-payment of rent only foreshadowed his lifelong cavalier attitude to debt.

Property deeds record how within months of his purchase of Terrett's Mill Rennison had mortgaged the premises for £400. To finance the Ladies' Bath and the building of the *Old England* he borrowed a further £200. In 1772 he transferred all his property, probably as a technical device, to his son Thomas but then borrowed more money to buy it back. Ten years later he remortgaged the premises, this time for £1,000, to enable him to repay his original debts. During this time he appears to have been constantly juggling his debts to keep his more pressing creditors at bay, one of the most persistent of whom was the carpenter who had worked on the *Old England*.[5] What is surprising is that, despite his reputation, which would be familiar to Bristol's business community, Rennison was always able to raise money. It may have been because his lenders believed that the Baths complex provided good security. Given his own proclivities, it was perhaps fitting that in his will, in which he left his property to his son and daughter, he made the wry proviso that if his son used the estate as security he should forfeit his share to his sister.

After the death of Thomas Rennison junior in 1802 and that of his sister Mary in 1806 the property passed to Mary's nephew, yet another Thomas Rennison, the third of that name. He proved to be no better at managing money than his grandfather. In 1818 he was adjudged bankrupt but continued to live at the *Old England* until 1825 when he moved to Stroud to resume his trade as a victualler.

Other members of the family were also living on the site. Sarah Rennison lived at 'Cold Bath House' between 1814 and 1825, and John Rennison had possession of the Baths and all the land and buildings adjoining the Mill Pond. In 1824 William Cox Rennison, the youngest son of Thomas Rennison junior, took control of the Rennison inheritance. He repaid all the debts on the estate,

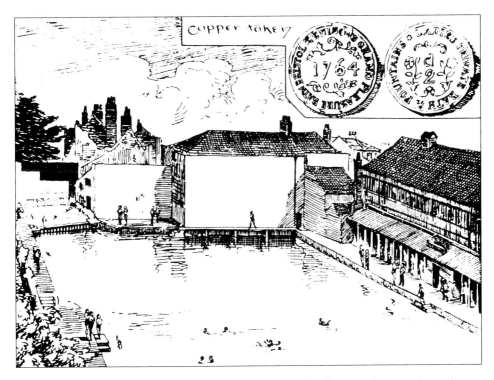

18 *Rennison's Baths sketched by S.J. Loxton c.1900 with admission tokens superimposed.*

with the interest that had accrued, to regain possession of the property his grandfather had mortgaged so freely. The conveyance deed listed the buildings that were on the site in 1824: the *Old England* tavern, with its garden and the Ice House under part of the tavern; the house adjoining the *Old England*; two Cold Baths; the Mill; the Mill House, and other adjacent buildings. There was also a large garden behind the Mill Pond called The Island, partly surrounded by water and planted with fruit and other trees. Finally there was the well and some outhouses in the courtyard adjoining the Brewhouse.

William Cox Rennison had assembled the property only to start selling off parts of it soon afterwards. In 1828 the *Old England* and its tea gardens were sold to William Peck, and in 1835 Richard Stratton paid £470 for the Island Garden, with the two houses standing there, one unfinished. This land was bought by Colston Girls' School in 1906; they demolished the houses and renamed the area The Pleasaunce. The Baths and the Mill appear to have remained in the Rennison family for rather longer. In 1845 the Health of Towns Commissioners reported that a Mr Rennison kept a cold swimming bath in the outparish of St Paul where the water was clear, good and in large quantity. The admission charge at that time was 2d., plus 1d. for a towel.[6] It is not clear when the Rennison family ceased to own them but the swimming baths continued to be known as Rennison's Baths for the duration of their life.

In 1875 Bristol Corporation Sanitary Authority began to acquire some of the buildings and land around the baths for road and drainage improvements. Then, in 1878, the proprietors of the baths offered to sell the whole premises of about an acre to the Corporation for £2,600. The Baths Committee withdrew from the negotiations but came back in 1891 to offer £1,500 for the baths which, they reported, were now free from ground rent. The purchase was completed and the baths were refurbished and reopened the following year. During the summer months the opening hours were 6a.m. to 8p.m. each day, including Sunday, extended to 9p.m. on Friday and Saturday. A reference in the Baths Committee Minutes in 1897 to the printing of handbills advertising skating shows that the baths were put to good use in winter too.[7]

In 1906 the Committee decided to build new baths at Rennison's at an estimated cost of £12,500, but deferred spending the money until they had 'considered the claims of more necessitous districts'.[8] That was the last that was heard of the scheme. In 1910 the Society of Merchant Venturers, trustees of Colston Girls' School, asked the Corporation to sell them a small piece of land behind the baths because they wanted to enlarge The Pleasaunce. The Corporation would only do so if the Merchant Venturers would agree to buy the baths and the adjacent buildings. This condition was rejected and the school then took a seven-year lease on the land. They eventually bought the freehold in 1922.

The baths were closed in 1916 as a wartime economy measure. They never reopened, although in April 1918 the St Andrew's Boy Scout troop was allowed to rent the premises for meetings. Three months later the entrance hall was declared to be in an unsafe and dangerous condition. The baths were roofed over, sold at auction in 1922 and used as a builder's yard until 1977. Then, not inappropriately, the Montpelier Health Centre was built on the site.

Rennison's House

Once Bristol Corporation had abandoned their plans to build new swimming baths to replace Rennison's, they appear to have lost interest in maintaining the other buildings they owned on the site. The tenants and neighbours of the properties, including the landlord of the *Old England*, frequently complained about their dilapidated state. All offers to purchase either the buildings or parts of the land were emphatically rejected by the Baths Committee. If they could not sell the complex as a whole they preferred to retain it and keep their options open for future development.

19 *A photograph of 1911 showing Rennison's Baths, the* Old England, *and Rennison's House between them.*

The building that caused the most controversy was a house that stood between the baths and the *Old England*. It was usually referred to as Rennison's House because it had been occupied by members of that family including, it was believed, by Thomas Rennison himself in the 18th century. It is difficult to be precise about its exact age. Items salvaged from it before it was demolished indicate a mid-17th-century date yet in the title deeds it is described as having been built by Thomas Melton, who did not buy the site until 1727. The possibilities are either that Melton had merely rebuilt an earlier house that had stood on this site and had retained some of its features or, bearing in mind his entitlement to materials from the old house at Cutler's Mill, he had incorporated these into his new house.

In 1903 the Corporation painted and repaired the house but by 1910, although still tenanted, it was reported to be in such poor condition that it would have to be pulled down. The Ashton Gate Brewery, which owned the *Old England*, was concerned about the damage to their property both from the dangerous state of the house and from the process of demolition. When Rennison's House was finally demolished in 1917 the museum removed the staircase, two doors and a door knocker, a cupboard and carved stone corbels which were 'suitable for exhibition in the Museum on account of their antiquity'. All the items except the staircase and one door have since disappeared. The staircase is stored in sections in the Industrial Museum and the door is cared for and displayed by the Bristol Savages in their meeting room.

20   *Door from Rennison's House now in the Bristol Savages' Wigwam.*

This door presents a problem. In its top corners are carved the initials T and R and in the centre panel the date 1663. It had been assumed that the initials were those of Thomas Rennison and that the date recorded his occupancy of the house. This cannot, of course, be the case for Thomas Rennison was not even born in 1663. The alternative explanations are: the initials are those of another person; they are a later addition to an earlier door; the date has been added to a later door. No one has yet been able to give a definitive answer but informed opinion favours the second explanation. Although this would fit neatly with the theory that some items in Rennison's House came from an older house, it remains hypothetical.

The Old England

Thomas Rennison's tavern, which has a long and continuous history of use as a public house, is still there. Although the interior has been altered the exterior remains much the same as it was in the 18th century. Its tea gardens and bowling green have gone but its sporting tradition is maintained by the tavern's cricket team, which practises in the nets behind.

When the adjoining house was demolished in 1917 it was found that its cellar extended underneath the *Old England*. During the 18th and early 19th centuries it had been used as an Ice House and rated as such. For some years it was let to William Bayston, a confectioner, who in the 1820s was the owner of numbers 9 and 10 (now 19 and 21) Picton Street. The *Old England* is now the sole surviving reminder of the long and rich history of Rennison's Baths.

Seven

THE GARDEN SUBURB
1791-1837

In the late 18th century the population of England began to grow quite rapidly and cities were expanding to meet the need for housing. In Bristol many of the more affluent families chose to move uphill to Clifton and across the slopes of Kingsdown in search of healthier air and open space. Others were attracted to the new suburb that was being created around Brunswick Square, north-east of the city. These residents soon started petitioning for a church which would add prestige to the neighbourhood and increase the value of their property. When St Paul's Church in Portland Square was consecrated in 1794, Montpelier and the other parts of Ashley that had been in the outparish of St James were transferred to the outparish of the new church.

Most of the planned house building was speculative, undertaken by builders, architects and financiers who worked together to secure sites that were likely to yield speedy and substantial profits. One of these groups identified some land in Montpelier as just such an attractive proposition. It was an area that offered the jaded city dweller all the advantages of rural living yet was only a short distance from the city's commercial centre. Access to it had recently been improved when the lane now known as Ashley Road had been made a turnpike road in 1786. So a plan to build good quality houses fronting this road seemed certain to succeed.

Ashley Place, 85-91 Ashley Road

In 1791 Peter Morris, a house carpenter, and his trustee, an apothecary named Robert Simpson, contracted to buy three acres, two roods and five perches of land in the fields called Wheatstubs (alias Chequer Ground) and Sparrowfurlong from Joseph Beck, the owner of the Ashley Estate.

In 1794 Morris undertook to lay out a minimum of £2,000 to build five or more 'good and substantial dwellinghouses' and within ten years to build more (later specified as six) houses to make 'a handsome uniform row' which would

45

21   *Ashley Place (85-91 Ashley Road). The architect, William Paty, had planned a terrace of 11 houses but only four were completed.*

be enclosed by a stone wall.[1] The five-storey, seven-bedroomed houses were to be built of good materials and to a high standard, with generous sized rooms, arched cellars and stabling. Strict covenants against any use that might detract from their value would be enforced with penalties. They should 'forever' be called Ashley Place and the street behind named Chequer Street, yet another reminder of the previous link with the *Chequer Inn.*

The builder's commitment to producing houses of quality was underwritten when Bristol's most eminent architect, William Paty, was taken into the partnership. Paty came from a well-known family of stone masons and carvers and gilders, and was the first Bristol architect to have a formal academic training at the Royal Academy Schools of Architecture. He had recently completed Christ Church in Broad Street, some houses in Great George Street (one is now the Georgian House) and Royal York Crescent. His design for Ashley Place, a row of houses linked by a single-storey annex containing the front door and crowned by a mansard roof, was a complete departure from the conventional terrace form. At about the same time Paty was planning houses of a similar style for Prince's Buildings, Clifton. Architectural historians have been intrigued by this pioneering design: Timothy Mowl regards Ashley Place as 'one of the most experimental and satisfying terraces in Bristol' although he does wrongly award the credit for it to the architect Daniel Hague.[2]

The terrace would have been even more impressive had it been completed as planned. However, by the end of 1792 there were distinct signs that the boom in speculative building was becoming unsustainable. Prices were rising, investors were wavering and credit was being restricted. Some grandiose building schemes were abandoned, including one for a terrace of 60 houses estimated to cost £60,000 near Ashley Down.[3] On 1 February 1793 France declared war on Britain and Holland and in the months following there was a flight of capital from the domestic market.

By 1794 Peter Morris had still only partially built four of the Ashley Place houses; in an effort to complete them he had borrowed £1,500 from Joel Gardiner and, in return, had leased to him the land reserved for the other projected houses. He also owed money to his architect and to his suppliers. He had no alternative but to allow himself to be declared bankrupt, along with many others in the building trade. All his personal effects were assigned to Paty and his other creditors, and he undertook to sell the land and houses 'to best advantage'.

They were auctioned at the Exchange Coffee House on 10 July 1795 and bought by Joel Gardiner for £1,500 (the capital sum he had invested in the property), which would be paid out of Morris's debt to him. The reasons for the auction were said to be: 'alterations in the times, stagnation of credit, scarcity of monies which resulted in the failures of builders of houses, most of which were going to decay'.[4] This was confirmed by commentators who visited Bristol around this time and

22 *Advertisement of 1942 which describes the accommodation at one of the houses.*

wrote of the tottering shells of roofless houses and the scene of desolation in the silent, deserted streets. There were over 500 houses in this state within the city and in the suburbs there were buildings left unfinished and schemes aborted. In Ashley Place the four partially built houses were eventually completed to specification but Joel Gardiner acknowledged that he was unlikely to be able to construct any more houses in the foreseeable future and reconveyed the land to the Beck family.

Upper Montpelier

There was a similar story of thwarted development on the hillside. In 1792 Edward Bearpacker leased four closes containing a total of 22 acres of land to Shurmer Bath, a maltster of 93 Stokes Croft. Bath agreed to pay an annual rent of £300 and to complete within five years 'so many good, substantial and uniform houses of stout brick and timber that should secure the £300 yearly income'.[5] By 1794, although Bath had completed several dwellings and was 'in great forwardness' with others, he could not afford to continue building. Bearpacker then offered to reduce the ground rent to £150 per annum until the war was over or the houses could be built. Before either of these objectives could be met both men had died, leaving their estates to their respective daughters. Because Shurmer Bath had breached the agreement, and was in considerable arrears with his rent, the land use reverted to the Bearpacker heiresses.

By that time, 1809, Shurmer Bath had laid out plots for houses and gardens, and 'several messuages and divers erections had been built thereon'. There

23 *Montpelier House/Villa, 94 Richmond Road.*

were also a few buildings 'near adjoining the Waggon Road leading from Stokes Croft to Ashley Barn'.[6] This was probably the future Cobourg Road, for in the 18th century two- and four-wheeled delivery vehicles were known as cobourgs. Although no documentary evidence has emerged to identify those houses that had been started but left unfinished, the owners of numbers 94 and 128 Richmond Road have detected structural differences which suggest they may have been built in two stages. A paper headed 'Cost of Montpelier Cottage' (128 Richmond Road), an itemised list of amounts

24 *131-133 York Road, formerly 13 and 14 Waterloo Place.*

spent to a total of £2,634, together with the rueful comment, 'I solemnly believe cost me more', was found in the Bristol Record Office.[7] It was undated but was in a bundle of other, unrelated, documents which were marked 1810.

The Bearpacker sisters sold a few plots privately[8] but most of the land was auctioned at the *Full Moon* in Stokes Croft on 17 August 1813.[9] The 61 lots, 59 of which were adjoining, were described as pleasantly situated, delightful spots for building or Pleasure Gardens, commanding the most magnificent and picturesque views of the city and adjacent counties. Plenty of good stone could be raised and bricks made on the premises. It seems that the purchasers were Bristol people who bought individual plots of land, sufficient for one or two houses or, at most, a short terrace. It was essentially small-scale development, undertaken by men with modest means and realistic ambitions.

As Ashmead's 1828 map of the area (Fig 1.) shows, all the building followed the existing narrow tracks that ran parallel up the slopes to the ridge of Ashley Hill. This set the pattern for future development so that it is still possible even on a modern map to trace the early field system and the routes up the hillside to Ashley Barn and Hooke's Mill. The new houses, which were mainly detached, were well spaced and designed to face south overlooking their large gardens and the meadows beside the Cutler's Mill Brook. The north-facing rear walls which were visible from the street were, in some cases, almost completely blank. Many more plots had been laid out but not yet built upon.

Most of the houses of this period have survived, although sometimes with unsympathetic alterations. The aptly named Ascension House (now Goodrich House) is still there at the top of York Road, as is Field House (116 St Andrew's Road). The Grove, which stood in large gardens just above it, was demolished for the building of Richmond Avenue. The two terraces that appear on the 1828 map: Waterloo Place (107-133 York Road) and Montague Buildings (119-29 'Richmond Road) remain intact.

Catherine Place and Wellington Place

Daniel Wait had bought the nine acres of Apesherd in 1800 but delayed development, probably awaiting signs of the end of the war. By 1812 he had built only two houses on the land, one for himself and the other for the Reverend Samuel Seyer, author of what is agreed to be the most scholarly history of Bristol and one of the finest town histories of the period. These adjoining houses can still be seen behind the garage showrooms at the corner of Bath Buildings and Cheltenham Road. He then engaged the architect James Foster, a pupil of William Paty, to divide the rest of the land into building plots. In 1812, possibly because his health was failing (he died the following year), Daniel Wait offered it for sale by auction:

> 35 lots of valuable land fronting the Stapleton Turnpike Road
> 22 lots of valuable land fronting the Gloucester Turnpike Road
> 20 lots of valuable land fronting the road leading to Rennison's Baths.
> The land is not liable to city taxes.[10]

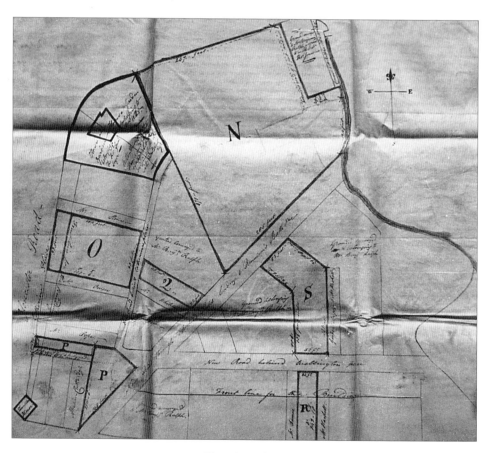

25 *Plan of Apesherd, 1816.*

26   *Wellington Place.*

Before the auction took place Benjamin Ralph, a Boot and Shoe Maker, and John Vaughan, a Gentleman, who was likely to have been financing the enterprise, agreed to buy the land for £6,200. The houses already built were excluded from the contract.[11] By 1816 builders had started work on a row of houses fronting the Gloucester Road (now Cheltenham Road) which was called Catherine Place. At the same time building was under way on the land facing the Stapleton Road. That terrace of houses became Wellington Place (now numbers 9-63 Ashley Road). Benjamin Ralph earmarked a large plot at the end of this terrace for his own house, which he named Wellington Lodge.

All these houses were to be fronted with freestone or the best front brick, with freestone door cases, window arches and sills. In Catherine Place, where the houses had only small front gardens, it was specified that the boundary walls dividing the plots should be no more than eight feet high.[12]

Wellington Place, unlike Ashley Place, was not planned as a unified whole, nor even with a uniform facade. The reason was that, although some of the

27   *View looking south from the road to Stapleton, by T.L.S. Rowbotham.*

larger plots were sold directly to owner-occupiers, the majority were leased to small builders. Each of them would then build two or three houses in a fashionable style, but within a narrow price range, that would sell quickly, often to investors who would then let them to tenants. Since the vast majority of the population in the early 19th century lived in speculatively built, rented houses, this was a lucrative business.

This practice was common but nowhere are its consequences more visible than in Wellington Place, which is a lively and diverse terrace of houses of mixed sizes and styles and striking individuality. Some have trellised balconies, most have traceried fanlights, one has a Venetian window and another an elegant bow-fronted façade. Secluded behind stone walls, they overlooked their long front gardens and the open fields that lay between them and Portland Square. In 1826 the artist Thomas Rowbotham, who lived in Catherine Place, painted the view from Wellington Place, which was of sheep grazing in the fields on which the Victorian houses of St Paul's would be built.[13]

Picton Street

A plan of Apesherd drawn for its new owners shows a track running through the middle of the site. It was marked 'New road through Apesherd Field leading to Rennison's Baths'.[14] This was the future Picton Street.

Building work started in 1816 and the street was largely completed by 1824. Although it contains some private houses it was planned as a shopping street to serve the burgeoning local community. The earliest surviving entry for a Picton Street resident in the parish records is the baptism in April 1823 of the child of Lucy and William Probert, a cheesemaker. By the following year, when their next child was baptised, William Probert was describing himself as a grocer.[15]

The other traders who established themselves in the new street were a butcher, baker, tailor, linendraper, shoemaker, plumber, carpenter, ironmonger, brushmaker and a beer retailer.[16] The last named may have been the proprietor of the *General Picton* public house, which was licensed to sell beer sometime before 1835.

The buildings themselves are modest but substantial. The materials, mostly redbrick Flemish Bond (alternate headers and stretchers in every course) and Bath stone for the door pilasters and hoods, are traditional. There are graceful doorways, framed by their canopies and fanlights, and a few original shop-fronts that have survived. The harmonious domestic scale of the street gives it an architectural unity that is emphasised by the stepped roofline rising gently up the hill. Most of the properties are three-storied with cellars. They were built with living accommodation for the proprietor and his family above and behind the shop, and long back gardens with space to grow vegetables and to keep chickens. The water supply came from a well in the cellar or garden, with the extra resource of a communal pump at the bottom of the street. The depth of the wells can be gauged from a report in the *Bristol Mercury* on 9 November 1830. A man named Legg, employed in sinking a well in Picton Street, unfortunately met his death in consequence of the earth giving way and falling in upon him.

There are two houses in the street that present a contrast to the domestic simplicity of the buildings around them. They are Picton House (No. 25) and Picton Lodge, formerly Villa (No. 45). The former is a detached double-fronted house that was built in 1816 for a Mr Langley, an accountant, who also bought property in Wellington Place.[17] The date for the building of Picton Lodge has to be arrived at by deduction. Since it is not on the Donne Map of 1826 but is on the Ashmead Map of 1828 it seems safe to assume it was built in 1827. It stands at right angles to the street, sited to take advantage of the view it would have had over Cutler's Mill Brook, which ran through meadows at the

28   *Picton Street, Bristol's only intact Georgian shopping street, photographed* c.*1970.*

29 *Picton Lodge/Villa, built in 1827.*

foot of its garden, to the Montpelier hillside. With its graceful bow front, its elaborate fanlight, and decorative stone urns on the coping stones, the house was obviously designed for someone with taste and money. It is not known who that person was but he did not live there for long. In 1836 the house became the office and residence of Robert Mercer, Clerk to the Clifton Poor Law Union and Registrar for St Paul's.

Next to Picton Lodge there is a lock-up or Charley Box. It is not shown on Ashmead's 1828 map but does appear on the map of 1832. It was built to house a nightwatchman or 'Charley' (the name is said to derive from Charles I, who reformed the watch system in London in 1640[18]) and to imprison law breakers overnight.

In the early 19th century methods of policing in England differed little from those of Tudor and Stuart times. Riot and disorder were dealt with by the military and individual breaches of law by parish constables and nightwatchmen. Bristol did not set up a municipal police force until 1836, and in outlying areas like Montpelier, still technically in Gloucestershire, there was scarcely any street lighting to deter crime and very few parish constables to arrest the criminals.

30   *Charley Box – the window is a later addition.*

So the Charley was given powers to arrest and confine overnight anyone who disturbed the peace and, if necessary, transfer him to the magistrates the following morning.

The accommodation in the Picton Street lock-up consisted of a very small room for the Charley and two barrel-vaulted cells, each measuring 12 feet by six feet, one of which still has its iron-studded door and a manacle on the wall. There was no window (the one in the frontage was inserted later) and only a small roof lantern for ventilation, which was covered by an iron grille. Below street level there were two more vaulted rooms with a squint in the dividing wall. It is not known when it ceased to be a lock-up but it would have been sometime after 1835, when Montpelier was incorporated within the Bristol city boundaries.

Upper and Lower Cheltenham Place

Possibly encouraged by the success of his Apesherd venture, Benjamin Ralph bought six acres of this land and promptly started work on houses in what was to become Upper and Lower Cheltenham Place. It was obviously a speculative development for in 1830 he was advertising the sale by auction of two newly built dwelling-houses, leasehold for 999 years, in Lower Cheltenham Place.[19] In

1833 he leased five of the houses to Jacob Cole, a shopkeeper, for £12 10s. per annum.[20] By 1834 there were 20 houses in Lower Cheltenham Place, although 10 of them were not occupied. By the same date he had completed, and sold or leased, 17 houses in Upper Cheltenham Place.

Ashley Road

Some of the land to the east of Ashley Place had been sold before 1825 to a builder named John Lawrence. He in turn had sold at least one plot to Thomas Graham, who had built a house there.[21] This may have been No. 117 Ashley Road, which bears a date of 1823. By 1828 there were still only three houses on this land but the 1846 map shows every plot from No. 117 to Sussex Place occupied by large houses. Imposing and built of high quality stone, they were obviously intended as homes for large and prosperous families. The remainder of the land in and behind Ashley Road, which had been bought by William Watson, a wine merchant, was not developed during this period.

Ashley Hill

Once the plan for the terrace of 60 houses on Ashley Down had been abandoned in 1792, no further interest was shown in building there until John Evans Lunell bought the farm lands of the Ashley Estate in 1825. Lunell, a respected businessman, churchman and local benefactor, saw the potential to create a pleasant residential area in what was then a remote rural spot. Since he lived on Ashley Hill he had a vested interest in maintaining the exclusive character of the neighbourhood so this was to be no speculative venture. His method was to lease plots of land to masons, who built for clients to whom Lunell conveyed the freehold when the houses were completed.

On the west side of Ashley Hill three detached houses were built on a close of land called Lower Ashley: Ashley Lodge (82 Cobourg Road) was built before 1828, Ashley Green in 1831 and Cumberland Villa (on the corner of Cobourg Road and Ashley Hill) around 1835. Ashley Lodge was the home of Robert Fletcher, an accountant and French Vice Consul in Bristol. In 1845 it was bought by Christopher Thomas, partner in the soap manufacturing firm, who lived there until 1849.

When Robert Fletcher left Ashley Lodge he moved only a short distance to a newly built house, which he named Ashley Green. John Lunell had sold the plot for this house in 1831 to a mason for £400. An architect, William Okely, was then engaged to produce a design to fit the challenging triangular site. A subsequent occupant of Ashley Green described the approach to the house: 'The grounds ran up as far as the railway line at Ashley Hill Bridge, there being a long drive, with an avenue of trees from the gates.'[22]

Cumberland Villa was another house set in pleasant, although less extensive, grounds. It had courts and gardens, a summer house, coach house, stable and an adjoining gardener's cottage.[23] All have been demolished or built over.

The grounds of Caer Brito (now number 12 Ashley Hill) on the east side of the hill have also been lost to building. They used to contain a tennis court, fishpond, grotto, greenhouse, vinery and kitchen garden, an Observatory Tower, and stabling with carriage drives at the front and side.[24] Higher up on Ashley Down three substantial detached houses, Holdenhurst, Down View and Glenfrome, were built overlooking long gardens that sloped down to the valley.

At the bottom of Ashley Hill some rather more modest houses were being put up, probably speculatively, in the newly named Sussex Place. John Lunell then linked this development to Ashley Hill, and opened up the area, by building a new road which he dedicated as a public highway.

St Paul's outparish rate books provide corroborative evidence of the number of houses that were built during this period and also enable a comparison to be made of their relative value. They confirm that Apesherd was the only part of the area to be fully developed within a decade. By 1824 virtually all the houses in Wellington Place, Catherine Place and Picton Street had been completed and occupied. By 1834 there were 32 houses in Richmond Road, 33 in York Road, 17 in Upper Cheltenham Place and 20 in Lower Cheltenham Place. Around Sussex Place there were seven houses (two of them unoccupied) and ten cottages.

The most highly rated properties were the four houses in Ashley Place; they were in fact the most valuable houses in the whole of St Paul's parish, which included the prestigious Portland Square. Ashley Court and the other large houses around Ashley Hill came slightly lower down the scale. Values in Wellington Place and Upper Montpelier varied according to the size of the property but, on average, they were moderate. The lowest were the cottages in Union Place and Picton Buildings, the lane behind Picton Street.

The Residents

The size and type of houses that were built determined the social structure of the area. Some of the wealthiest local businessmen gravitated towards the large houses around Ashley Hill. The fact that in later decades at least four Lord Mayors of Bristol had private residences there indicates that its reputation as a desirable location was retained for some time. Ashley Place and Upper Montpelier appealed to the professional and entrepreneurial classes: clergyman, surgeon, attorney, merchant and bookseller are some of the occupations given in the parish records.

The provision of a wider range of housing on Apesherd guaranteed a social mix of residents that would be more representative of society as a whole, although the extremes of wealth and poverty were unlikely to be found there. The larger houses in Wellington Place were occupied by professional people or by the successful self-employed tradespeople; the smaller by people of more modest means. Amongst those who lived there in the 1830s were R.S. Pope, the prolific Bristol architect and city surveyor; John Perry, who owned the coach-making business in Stokes Croft; and Benjamin Ralph, the bootmaker whose rewarding property ventures now entitled him to describe himself as 'a gentleman'. Accountants, a title which in the 19th century was usually applied to anyone doing clerical work, were found in every type of house.

Picton Street housed mainly the shopkeepers who traded there, but also those who lived in the private terraced houses whose occupations were either clerical or skilled manual. The cottages in Picton Lane had a surprisingly diverse range of tenants in the 1820s such as a schoolteacher, a carpenter and a coachman, but by the middle of the century they were more likely to be occupied by servants or labourers.

A number of artists, some of whom became well known, moved into the area during this period, probably attracted by its varied and interesting landscape. T.L.S. Rowbotham, who lived at 14 Catherine Place (now 150 Cheltenham Road), painted a number of local scenes. E.V. Rippingille RA, the narrative painter and prominent member of the Bristol School of Artists, lived at 22 Wellington Place (now No. 51 Ashley Road) in 1830. At about the same time there were two painters of miniatures and a 'scenic artist' at addresses around Rennison's Baths.

Street Names

The names of the streets and houses of Montpelier reflect the patriotic fervour that was sweeping the country at the time they were being built. After his defeat of Napoleon at Waterloo in 1815 the Duke of Wellington became a national hero. Throughout Britain, and much of Europe, he was venerated to a degree that was little short of idolatry.

In 1816 he came to Bristol to receive the freedom of the city. Since that was the year when building work started on Apesherd it was almost inevitable that he would be commemorated there by Wellington Place, Lodge and Cottage. Catherine Place had already been named, possibly after Catherine Wait, daughter of the earlier owner of the land. So, that left only the new shopping street to be given a name associated with the great victory.

The name Picton is so ubiquitous in and around Picton Street that it is often assumed that the General of that name had a close connection with the

31   *Ashley Lodge, 82 Cobourg Road. Between 1845 and 1849 it was the home of Christopher Thomas, owner of one of the largest soap-making firms in the country.*

area. In fact his only connection with Bristol stemmed from 1783 when he suppressed an incipient mutiny of soldiers in his regiment which was temporarily billeted in the city while awaiting disbandment after the American War of Independence. He was a Welshman from Pembrokeshire, a career soldier who had a chequered army career. When he was Military Governor of Trinidad it was alleged that he allowed a woman to be tortured. At his court martial he was cleared but the verdict was controversial.[25] His future reputation was assured, however, by the bravery he showed in battle and the manner of his death at Waterloo. When he was badly injured by a musket ball he ordered his servant to strap him up and tell no one. He fought on for two days until, leading a final charge against the French, he was shot in the head and killed. His portrait hangs on the wall above No. 6 Picton Street, the former *General Picton* public house.

Ashmead's 19th-century maps are inconsistent in their naming of the roads that run up the hill to Montpelier but property deeds of the early 1800s generally refer to them as Upper and Lower New Roads. The houses that were built after 1815 were given appropriately patriotic names which were later transferred to the roads in which they stood. York Road and York House honoured the second son of George III, although the Grand Old Duke's reputation during the Napoleonic Wars was somewhat less than heroic. Richmond Place was named after the Duke of Richmond, a veteran of the Peninsular Campaign. Waterloo Place was yet another reminder of the famous battle.

By the end of the Georgian period Montpelier was a place in its own right. Instead of being subsumed in Ashley it had become an instantly recognisable, if still relatively isolated, suburb. The residents of the villas on the southern slopes enjoyed both their elegant homes and the tranquillity of their semi-rural surroundings. Those who lived in Lower Montpelier had less open space but, despite the intensive development in and around Picton Street, they still had a rural outlook. Nearly all the houses had large gardens and there was fertile land and foliage in every direction. Even Stokes Croft, that busy built-up route into the city, was tree-lined. There were nursery gardens on the ground between Cheltenham Road and Rennison's Baths and from there the Cutler's Mill Brook ran through the meadows to Sussex Place.

The old tracks up the hill were improved, and kept in repair by the residents of the adjacent houses, but their line remained unchanged. The only innovations for ingress and egress occurred on the fringes of the area. These were the new line of road that was made from Stokes Croft to Cutler's Mill in 1824 and the public road that opened up a route from Sussex Place to Ashley Hill around 1830. The old turnpike stood at the top of Ashley Road then, once development was under way, a new gate was erected at Bath Buildings, no doubt to prevent travellers evading the toll by cutting through Picton Street. In 1823-4 the combined income from these two gates was £1,841. When the city boundaries were extended in 1832 they were replaced by a new gate and tollhouse at Cutler's Mill, close to the present railway bridge.

By this time it was becoming clear that the anomaly of Montpelier's position as a suburb edging physically ever closer to Bristol yet still legally part of Gloucestershire would have to be addressed. It was resolved by a series of political and social reforms which brought Montpelier, and other suburbs, firmly under the aegis of Bristol. The first came in June 1832 when the Parliamentary Reform Bill, agitation for which had provoked the violent Bristol Riots of the previous year, became law. As a result the city's parliamentary boundaries were redrawn to include, *inter alia*, Montpelier. It also meant that male householders with property worth £10 would be entitled to vote for Bristol's parliamentary candidates.

This was followed in September 1835 by the Municipal Corporations Act, under which the city's municipal boundaries were made conterminous with its parliamentary borders. Local wards were created for which councillors were to be elected by ratepayers of three years' standing. Montpelier was brought within the St Paul's ward.

Those Montpelier residents who were poor, sick or unemployed were affected by one of the major social reforms of this period. Since the 16th century, responsibility for providing relief for such people had rested with the individual parishes, resulting in services of very uneven quality. Under the Poor Law Amendment Act of 1834 an attempt was made to standardise provision by bringing the parishes together in a union which would operate through an elected Board of Guardians. The in and out parishes of St Paul's came under the Clifton Poor Law Union, which had its office in Picton Lodge.

Eight

Victorian Montpelier
The Early Years 1837-1860

During the first decades of the new Queen's reign Bristol's economy was relatively static. Census returns for this period show the city's population growing more slowly than at any time in the 19th century. In Montpelier this was reflected in a sudden decline in house building, especially noticeable after the earlier spurt of activity. From contemporary maps it seems that the only significant additions to the housing stock at this time were a row of houses built on the nursery land in Bath Buildings and two terraces, one in Richmond Road and the other in the lower part of York Road. Yet when a large parcel of ground on the west side of Cheltenham Road came on the market there was a great flurry of building activity. This disparity can probably be explained by the fact that, whereas in Montpelier all the prime sites had already been taken, the new suburb of Cotham had ample space for the large detached and semi-detached villas still being sought by affluent families who wanted to live within easy reach of the city.

There was, however, some land to the east of Cheltenham Road where prime sites could be found. The Cutler's Mill Estate remained primarily agricultural although there was some small-scale industrial use of the land, for quarrying and for a 'manufacture of cotton balls'. The extension of the city's northern boundary and the new, improved road access should have made this area potentially attractive to developers. Yet, for unknown reasons, but maybe because they foresaw a lack of immediate demand, large investors do not appear to have been interested. Instead it was small local entrepreneurs who seized what must have seemed a golden opportunity.

In 1834 William Williams, a coachmaker and timber merchant of Lampblack (Arley) Hill, leased from James Martin 11 acres called Fairfield for 99 years at an annual rent of £100. Under this arrangement the builder was able to acquire the land without capital outlay while the owner soon recouped the value of his land.[1] Williams had already obtained some land in Bath Buildings in this way.

He covenanted to build on Fairfield '10 more dwellinghouses or other buildings' on which he would spend at least £5,000. At the end of the lease the land was to be surrendered to Martin's heirs.[2] In 1839 Williams sub-let a plot of this land to Ann Naish, described as a widow, who undertook to build on it within two years 'no more than four houses not of less class than the three houses in or opposite Bath Buildings in Maddocks Lane,[3] lately erected by Williams'.[4] Ann Naish was the widow of a member of a prosperous family of Hosiers, Glovers and Cotton Ball Makers who had recently begun to invest in land in and around Montpelier. St Paul's parish rate books for 1834 show Mrs Naish as the ratepayer for a house, a factory and six gardens in Upper Montpelier. This factory, which made cottons balls, was in the garden of the family's house between what is now Richmond Avenue and Fairfield Road.[5]

Mrs Naish appears to have built only one house, Fairfield Cottage, on her plot. Its garden may have been the site of the factory but, since the family owned more that one house in Montpelier, it is difficult to be certain. William Williams built numbers 1 and 2 Fairfield (now Clifton) Villas near the top of St Andrew's Road but there is no evidence that he started any more houses before his death in 1866.

In 1844 Edward Martin sold nine acres of the estate to James and Samuel Derham for £2,475. They were Boot and Shoe Manufacturers who were establishing their first business in Wrington, Somerset. When, some years later, they expanded and opened a factory in St James's Barton they became one of Bristol's major employers. They seem to have delayed developing this land for almost 40 years, by which time they had acquired the rest of the Cutler's Mills Estate.

The Churches

The domestic property market may have been dormant at this time but the demand for ecclesiastical buildings was buoyant. At least 19 new churches were built in the Bristol suburbs during these years, not to mention the large number of chapels for the nonconformists. In St Paul's outparish two churches were built within two years and the community of Montpelier divided between them.

St Paul's Church had been built to accommodate 1,500 people but by 1840 the combined population of the in and out parishes had grown to 15,000. In April of that year the Church Building Society, which had been established to provide additional churches 'for the middle and lower classes',[6] gave £1,000 for the erection of a new church in Montpelier. Two sites were nominated for the church, one at Rennison's Baths, the other at Ashley Place. St Paul's Vestry had reservations about the latter, which was 'too near the mother church and remote from the most populous parts of the parish'.[7] By March 1842 it had been decided that two churches would be needed, one to serve Lower Montpelier and the other Upper Montpelier and part of Horfield parish. The site for the former was laid out 'in Stokes Croft Nursery Grounds, opposite Ashley Place':[8] it had been given to the bishop by W. Brigstocke Esq. The church, dedicated to St Barnabas, was consecrated in September 1843, on which occasion it was 'crowded to excess by a highly respectable congregation'.[9] The church was built on stone vaulting about seven feet high which was intended as a crypt for burials. Only one body was buried there before all such interments were prohibited by Act of Parliament. The Parsonage, which is still there, was built of Bath stone and had seven bedrooms and two living rooms which were to be used as parish rooms.[10] After attending a service in St Barnabas in

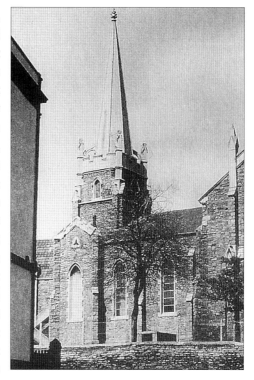

32 *St Barnabas's Church, consecrated 1843, demolished 1970.*

February 1844, Joseph Leech, the editor of the *Bristol Times* and indefatigable church visitor, wrote, 'the church is situated in Ashley Road … though not an aristocratic yet a most comfortable neighbourhood, the inhabitants being mainly of the middle class'.[11]

The other local church was built behind Rennison's Baths, facing what is now St Andrew's Road. The financial implications of building this second church seem to have disturbed the St Paul's Vestry: when asked to subscribe to the building fund they replied that they would have 'cheerfully' done so had they not needed all the money for their own repairs. However, shortly afterwards, for some unexplained reason, they became actively hostile to the new church, refusing to attend either the laying of its foundation stone in 1843 or its consecration two years later, declining 'further interference in the business'.[12]

St Andrew's Church was cruciform, built in the Early English style, with a 60 ft high tower and a steep roof. Its carved oak communion table was said to be modelled on one in Cologne Cathedral. The organ was supplied by Jacob Keeler of No. 1 (now 41) Picton Street, maker of church, chamber and barrel organs.

33   *St Andrew's Church, consecrated 1845, demolished 1969.*

The boundary between the two parishes followed the course of Cutler's Mill Brook. Picton Street was in the anomalous position of straddling the brook and therefore had its residents divided between the parishes, with the occupants of nos. 1-39 allocated to St Barnabas's and those of nos. 2-49 to St Andrew's.

Another religious building in a very different style made a distinctive contribution to the local landscape during this period. Arley Chapel in Cheltenham Road was built for the Congregationalists and opened in 1855. It was designed by the architects Foster and Wood in the Italianate style and built at a cost of £4,000. With its semi-circular portico and flanking Corinthian columns, it was obviously designed to have maximum visual impact on this prominent corner site.

Education

Before 1870 there was no national system of secular education in England, the only available schooling being provided by religious, philanthropic or private bodies. In Montpelier a number of private schools were advertising for pupils as early as the 1820s. The 'Preparatory School for Young Gentlemen' in Ashley Hill and 'Mrs Cottrill's and Miss Selkirk's Establishment' at 1 Catherine Place, where 'Young Ladies are educated',[13] may have been as superior as they claim but standards in these schools were variable and entirely unregulated. The best Dame Schools taught reading, sewing and other domestic skills but the worst provided little more than a childminding service.

Those children from poorer homes who were actually sent to school, and most were not, generally attended church elementary schools, one of which was opened in Montpelier in 1850, on a site adjoining St Andrew's Church. The land, measuring 190½ft by 60ft, was given by Joseph and James Martin, owners of the Cutler's Mills Estate, in July 1848 to be used 'for the education of the children of labouring, manufacturing and other poorer classes in the District of St. Andrew, Montpelier and as a residence for a schoolmaster and mistress'.[14] The site for the school, adjoining schoolhouse and playground lay behind the church and the burial ground, which was entered from St Andrew's Road. The land on the other side of the church was reserved for the proposed Parsonage which was not built until 1862. St Andrew's School was one of the many schools founded by the National Society for Promoting the Education of the Poor in the Principles of the Church of England, generally known as National Schools. They concentrated on teaching the '3Rs' and on giving religious instruction. Pupils were grouped according to ability and taught in a single classroom by the monitorial method, i.e. a teacher instructed the older pupils who then passed on what they had learned to the younger children. In 1833 the government began to give grants for buildings and for the payment of pupil teachers. In 1862 a system of payment by results was introduced whereby funding became dependent on pupils' attendance and examination results. When St Andrew's School opened, 73 boys and 61 girls were registered of whom 58 and 40 respectively attended daily. Their parents paid a weekly fee of 2d.[15] In 1859 the school was enlarged by the addition of a gallery that could seat a further 60 children.

Sanitation

When Montpelier and other suburbs were being built there seems to have been a general assumption that the increasing need for fresh water would be met by the customary means: the storage of rainwater, wells and communal pumps.

The larger houses were provided with their own wells and the smaller terraced houses shared a well with a neighbour and used the communal pump. The potential for conflict over this shared access was acknowledged in property deeds which usually specified water rights and responsibilities for the upkeep of supplies.

The same assumption was made about the disposal of water and sewage. Rainwater was carried to the rivers by the tributary streams, which, in the case of Montpelier, was the Cutler's Mill Brook which flowed into the River Frome. Household waste went into cesspools which might be connected to rudimentary sewers but more often just expelled their contents into the street. This dependence on the efficacy of river disposal may have been acceptable when the population was small and when the daily ebb and flow of a tidal River Frome could carry away the waste. Difficulties arose as the number of suburban households increased and were compounded by the building of the Floating Harbour in 1809, when the Frome, which flowed into it, was effectively sealed off from the tide. The diverting of the river into the New Cut in 1825 only partially improved matters for the highest tides alone could penetrate far enough to clear the waste efficiently.

By the 1830s it was becoming obvious that the insanitary state of Bristol and other large towns was a huge problem. In 1831 the first outbreak of cholera in Britain led to research which produced evidence for the link between sanitation and public health. A Royal Commission, set up to investigate the state of large towns, visited Bristol. Its report, issued in 1845, was searingly critical of the city, a place of 'squalor, dirt and disease'.[16] Its water supply was the worst in the country and its mortality rate the third highest in England. The report highlighted the hazard caused by the discharge of raw sewage into the Frome and the Floating Harbour. The City Council acted speedily to remedy the lack of clean water, endorsing a scheme to bring into the city a new supply from a spring in Mendip. Predictably, piped water, like other amenities, was brought to the suburbs first and only later to the urban poor. Clifton and Westbury-on-Trym were early beneficaries, then in 1846 water pipes were laid in Picton Street. A charge of 2d. per week was levied on each household for this new amenity.

Less urgency was shown in dealing with drainage, but in 1849, after an outbreak of cholera in Bristol had killed 444 people, a government inspector, G.T. Clark, was appointed to investigate the problems. In his report Clark drew attention to Montpelier's plight. Upper Montpelier 'though covered with superior houses is without drainage except into cesspools'.[17] These cesspools expelled their contents into the open gutter thus exposing neighbouring wells to the risk of contamination. Lower Montpelier had some sewers, probably inadequately

34   *Interior of St Andrew's Church.*

constructed – a few were found to run backwards – but these only drained into the open ditch that ran through Ashley Vale to Baptist Mills and thence to the River Frome. Not only was the stench from this ditch 'unsupportable' but, Clark alleged, some people had died from fevers caught from it. Of Cutler's Mill Brook he said, 'the stream is particularly filthy and irregular. Upon it is a large dirty pool, at the back of Rennison's Baths, which it, until recently, supplied with water.'

Following this report, in 1851 the City Council set up a Local Board of Health to deal with the issues it had raised. The Board's main proposal was that all sewage should in future be discharged into the River Avon and none into the Frome. To do this trunk sewers should be built at right angles to the existing small sewers and streams to intercept the sewage before it reached the river. They would then discharge the sewage down river at a point where the Avon was well clear of the urban district.

Work started in Montpelier in 1859 to lay a branch sewer along the existing roads and up Ashley Hill. That was followed by the construction of a main sewer up the whole length of the Cutler's Mill Brook. In all 80 miles of sewers were built in the city. The consequence of this and other measures taken to improve sanitation was that by 1869 *The Times* was praising Bristol for transforming itself 'from nearly the most unhealthy to nearly the most healthy town in Great Britain'.[18] However, the sewerage scheme, ambitious and effective as it seemed at the time, did not resolve all of Montpelier's, or Bristol's, drainage problems. It would take a further three decades, and two major floods, to secure the necessary radical solution.

Lighting

Although Bristol was one of the first cities to introduce gas lighting in its streets, it was slow to extend supplies to the outer areas. Bristol Gas Light Company was formed in 1815. By 1817 all the principal streets in the city had gas lamps and some public lighting was installed in Clifton by 1824. Almost 30 years later, in 1851, the City Council agreed to invite tenders for lighting the streets of the suburbs. Although there is no documentary evidence to show when Montpelier's streets were first lit, it is likely to have been soon after this date.

There is another reason why Montpelier just may have received some priority when gas pipe laying contracts were awarded. In 1857 Ebenezer Breillat, the chief engineer of the Bristol Gas Company, built two houses in Cobourg Road and moved into one of them. Appropriately enough he named them after two pioneers of the gas industry. Murdock Villa, where he lived, recalled William Murdock, and Winsor Villa the German entrepreneur, Frederick Albert Winsor.[19]

Nine

URBANISATION
1860-1900

In contrast to the comparative sluggishness of the previous two decades, the 1860s and '70s were marked by unprecedented growth in the population of Bristol and its suburbs. This was partly due to a countrywide excess of births over deaths but also to the migration of people from the country to the town. A series of bad harvests and competition from cheaper imported wheat grown on the American prairies drove many farmers into bankruptcy and labourers off the land to seek employment in towns. Between 1870 and the end of the century 300,000 agricultural labourers left the countryside.[1]

For farmworkers from Gloucestershire and Somerset Bristol presented attractive opportunities. The city was relatively prosperous and there were prospects of employment in the growing number of small, diverse local industries. Thanks to the reforms in sanitation, health and living conditions had greatly improved. This surge in population led to a revival in speculative building and it was this that, by the end of the century, would transform Montpelier from an airy green suburb to a densely developed part of the inner city.

Housing

Some of the new houses were built between the Georgian villas and terraces, others on what had, until then, been meadows or gardens. Establishing the sequence of building during this period is relatively easy for since 1851, as part of the public health reforms, all plans for sewers, drains and houses had had to be submitted to the City Engineer for approval. Between 1858 and 1867, in addition to the plans submitted for building on sites in the older roads, there were applications to build in several new locations. Albert Park, Albert Park Place, Chancery (now Brook) Road, Albany Road and East and West Grove were all developed at this time. In the mid-1870s the land below Cutler's Mill Brook was laid out for the building of Banner Road and Norrisville Road.

Shaftesbury Avenue followed in the late 1880s. The building of Wellington Avenue at the bottom of the hill and of the houses in and around Fairfield Road at the top completed the residential development of Montpelier. According to the Building Indexes 742 houses were erected in the suburb between 1860 and 1900.

This hunger for building land led to the loss of some historically interesting houses, regardless, it seems, of their condition, and purely for their site value. Montpelier Farm, Ashley Court and The Grove, a house of which nothing is known except that Richmond Avenue was built on its gardens, were all demolished and, as Latimer says, 'converted into building plots, the demand for which was then very active'.[2]

The long delayed development of the Cutler's Mill Estate finally started at around this time. In 1877 the Derham family signed a contract with the owners of the land which committed them to expend £28,320 on 'good, substantially built dwellinghouses' to be completed before 1884.[3] As was becoming the norm for this estate, there was a delay in starting the project but work did begin within the decade. A few of these houses were built in St Andrew's Road but the vast majority were sited on the land north of there. In a break with the past, and in recognition of its parochial links, the new development was called the St Andrew's Estate.

When the turnpike tolls were abolished in 1867 the Cutlers Mill's gate and tollhouse, together with the other 14 gates in the city, were removed. The following year an application was submitted for eight houses to be built on the site, fronting Cheltenham Road. They are still there, although now converted to shops.

The type of houses that were being built during this period not only reflected the developers' estimation of current demand in each area of the city but also determined the future social composition of those areas. So, while the villas in the new outer suburbs of Clifton and Redland were designed to appeal to the affluent and aspiring middle class, the much more modest houses that were springing up in Montpelier and other inner suburbs were intended for the lower middle class. The differences were not limited to size and substance; in architectural style the developments were poles apart. The detached and semi-detached houses in the outer suburbs were built in an eclectic mixture of styles, with a bias towards the gables and highly ornamented façades of the fashionable neo-Gothic. In the inner suburbs in the 1860s and '70s house building continued along traditional lines: economical classical terraces with uniform, even austere, façades. Houses of this type, sometimes called sub-Georgian, can be seen in the streets around Brook Road. As Andor Gomme says, when it is simple and seemly this design 'is certainly not to be complained of'.[4] The radical change

35 *Oast House and adjacent Malt House, built in 1876, now converted to housing.*

came in the mid-1880s when what we now regard as typical Victorian houses, bay-windowed and with pre-moulded surface decoration, began to appear in Montpelier.

Shopping

The shops in Picton Street continued to supply the daily needs of local residents. In the 1870s there were three grocers, two greengrocers, two butchers and a dairy. There was the *General Picton* public house at no. 6 and the *Robert Burns* at no. 54. The *Crown and Dove* at no. 19 may have been a third, although, since it also served groceries, it is more likely to have been a 'jug and bottle' shop. The Charley Box had by then acquired a window to enable its new occupant, a watchmaker, to carry on his business. Local people could pay their taxes and register births and deaths at Picton Lodge although they had to wait until 1892 for a post office to be opened at no. 48.

By the late 1860s it had become clear that there was scope for more, and larger, shops to serve the growing population. In 1867 work started on the construction of four shops with large storage cellars on a prominent site on the corner of Ashley Road and Cheltenham Road. By 1870 the completed shops,

36 · *Shops at the corner of Cheltenham Road and Ashley Road known as Golden Cross. They were built in the 1860s; the photograph shows them in 1907.*

named 'Golden Cross', were occupied by a chemist, a fishmonger, a draper and a jeweller. Next door stood the *Berkeley Castle* public house, then the *Black Horse Inn*, and beyond them some houses that had given up their front gardens to become shops. Behind Golden Cross, on a site in Ashley Road now occupied by the Salvation Army shop, were the greenhouses of the local nurseryman.

Most streets had a corner shop and rows of shops were built in Sussex Place, Richmond Road and St Andrew's Road. The proprietor of one of those in St Andrew's Road, Mr B. Pullin, advertised himself as 'a maker of high class boots and shoes on anatomical principles'.[5] He was so successful that in 1879 he moved to much larger premises in Stokes Croft. There were at least 12 public houses, including the new *Montpelier Hotel* which had been built for passengers using the nearby railway station.

Local Industries and Employment

From information obtained from census returns and street directories it seems that local people were engaged in a variety of occupations. This pattern mirrored the diversified economy of Bristol itself, which was not, and never had been, entirely dependent on any one industry.

Boot and shoe making was an occupation frequently given. This is not surprising because it was a thriving industry with a strong local base, especially around St Paul's. In the early 1870s a total of 18 houses in Portland Square were converted to boot and shoe factories, an indication not only of the current demand but also of the rapid decline of this formerly highly prestigious area. These firms were quite minor in comparison with Derham Brothers, which occupied a seven-storey building in St James Barton and had a permanent work-force of 1,500, augmented at peak periods by another 500 casual workers. To meet the demand for cheap footwear they introduced mass production techniques, but as late as the 1880s some stitching and cutting was still being done at home by outworkers.

Coach making was another common occupation. Many would live within walking distance of their work at the carriageworks of T. and J. Perry in Stokes Croft. Their first factory had opened on the site in 1804; then, after it was destroyed by fire, the distinguished architect E.W. Godwin was commissioned to design a new factory and showrooms which were completed in 1862. A variety of carriages from stylish Broughams to everyday dog carts was displayed in the showrooms' open-fronted arcades.

Stokes Croft Brewery was another major local employer providing work for both manual and clerical staff. It was one of the oldest brewing firms in the country and occupied extensive premises on the corner of City Road and Stokes Croft.

In Upper Montpelier it seems that Mr Naish was still working a cotton loom in his garden around 1860, although it is not known whether he employed many people. Then, in 1876, Mr Piller who lived in Rockley Villa in Fairfield Road built a malthouse and oasthouse in a nearby field.

The growth in the population was a great stimulus to the building trade: *Kelly's Bristol Directory* of 1883 lists 180 building firms in the city. No doubt many of these were quite small but two of the major firms were locally based: William Cowlin and Son were in St Paul's, and Stephens Bastow occupied a site in Bath Buildings. Founded in 1839, Stephens Bastow was a highly regarded company which won contracts, against national competition, for building and restoring churches, for large commercial buildings and for the Lyric Theatre in London. Many of these projects were carried out with the leading architects of the day, such as Pugin and Waterhouse. Bath Buildings was a highly convenient spot for such a business for it had excellent transport links. There was ample space on the site, which measured almost half an acre, for all their workshops and a large covered timber store from which they could supply other smaller builders. In the 1890s one of the proprietors, Mr G. Stephens, lived close by in Arley House, 174 Cheltenham Road.[6]

In the service sector, the occupation of railway porter appeared for the first time in local census returns of 1881. The opening of public transport links to the area would create many new employment opportunities for local residents during the coming decades. In addition to all the shopkeepers there were many other self-employed tradesmen, craft workers and artists who ran their businesses in and from their own homes. Typical of these were the two spinster ladies who made and sold straw hats and bonnets in their house at number 16 Picton Street. In the same street there were a number of fly proprietors who earned their living by hiring out horse-drawn vehicles. Given the amount of good, accessible stabling in the nearby rear lanes, this was an obvious occupation to follow.

Although the social balance had been changed by the influx of generally lower-middle-class occupants to the new houses, the area remained relatively mixed. The older, larger houses were still home to people who worked in commerce or the professions. It is noticeable how many of them were the owners of local businesses who had chosen to live close to their workplace. Having servants was not just the prerogative of the rich; residents of quite modest houses would often employ a daily servant, who might live nearby. Families in the larger houses were more likely to have live-in servants, many of whom came from the Blue Maids Orphanage in Ashley Hill, where they would have been well trained in domestic skills.[7]

Transport

On 1 October 1874 Montpelier railway station was opened on the first section of the Clifton Extension Railway. The line was built and operated jointly by the Great Western and Midland Railway companies, mainly as a link to their other services into and out of Bristol. Initially the line terminated at Clifton Down yet, even on this very limited route, there were 46 trains (23 each way) running every day. In 1885, after the opening of the Clifton Down tunnel, the line was extended to Avonmouth. The land required for the building of the railway was taken almost entirely from the Cutler's Mill Estate. A schedule of land ownership was prepared in the 1860s. It listed the owners, lessees and occupiers of the affected land and shows, predictably, that the Martin family were the main landowners and that the executors of William Williams were the main lessees.[8] They, or their successors, were paid compensation of £1,150 per acre by the railway companies when they finally acquired the land in 1871.[9]

37   *Montpelier Station, opened in 1874.*

The construction of the tunnel, steep embankments and the arched railway bridge across Cheltenham Road transformed the local landscape and there were those who protested against the loss of the open green fields, which they saw as the lungs of the area. Others, no doubt, would welcome the wider employment and business opportunities that would be opened up through the good rail connections. The railway also brought increased choice in leisure activities. It became much easier to take a day trip to the country or seaside. During holiday months special excursion trains proved very popular with families. In the summer of 1888 Montpelier Station issued 627 adult and 1,038 child day return tickets to Weston-super-Mare, which yielded an income of £75 6s. So many people wanted to travel to the 1886 Bath and Wells Show on the Downs that an extra four porters, one clerk and 12 ticket collectors had to be brought in to help the regular staff. Staff were also kept busy with goods traffic; in 1889 they handled a total of 3,184 parcels.[11]

The line was double track with two largely uncovered platforms, both more than 400 feet long, linked by an iron footbridge. There was a resident stationmaster who lived above the waiting rooms on the (surviving) down platform. In 1895, in response to a petition, the railway companies agreed to extend the roof over each platform and to improve the waiting facilities on both sides. It is recorded that in February 1885 the railway committee decided

38   *The* Montpelier Hotel *in St Andrew's Road was built to serve railway passengers.*

the name of the station board should have one 'l', not two.[12] In 1891 the railway companies were reprimanded by St Paul's Vestry, who sent them a memorial 'objecting on grounds of convenience and morality to their leaving Station Road in darkness when no trains are running'.[13]

The railway had not been long established before another form of transport was introduced into the area. The Bristol Tramways Company opened their first tramline between Perry Road and Redland in 1875; then, soon afterwards, in response to public demand, they began to extend the service on other key routes. Trams came to Montpelier in 1880 on a route from the Horsefair, along Stokes Croft and Cheltenham Road, continuing to the terminus at Egerton Road, Horfield. Another connection was made in 1892 when tram lines were laid along City Road to link Sussex Place to Stokes Croft.

The first of these open double-decker trams were horse-drawn, then in 1881 came a trial period during which the Horfield line was worked by steam. This experiment was rapidly abandoned after it proved to be not only noisy and dirty but also uneconomic. From 1895 electrification, by means of overhead wires, was gradually introduced so that by 1900 the whole system was powered by electricity. It was this rapid, clean and, above all, cheap new mode of transport that changed the working, shopping and leisure activities of the ordinary people in Montpelier, and other areas of Bristol, at the end of the 19th century.

Education

Until 1872 St Andrew's National School was the major provider of elementary education for the children of Montpelier. There were still a number of Dame Schools in the area, including three in Picton Street, one of which was called 'Miss Taylor's Seminary'.[14] Given the size of their premises these must, necessarily, have been very small schools. Then, in 1870, appeals were made in the local press for funds to build a school to serve St Barnabas's parish, which included the lower part of Montpelier. In 1872 this school, designed by the architect J.A. Clarke, was opened on a site next to the church but with its entrance in the recently made City Road. Whilst it would draw many of its pupils from the families moving into the newly built houses in St Paul's, this extra school must also have relieved some of the pressure on St Andrew's, although the extent of this cannot be demonstrated because the relevant admission records have been lost.

Coinciding, as it did, with the passing of legislation which, for the first time, provided secular, rate-supported elementary schools, the building of St Barnabas's School may have been designed to prevent a secular school opening in the area. The 1870 Education Act had been strongly opposed by members of the City Council and by some Anglicans who 'feared it would train a generation for infidelity and immorality'.[15] Despite this opposition a School Board was immediately set up to administer the Act. It carried out a census which revealed that only one-third of all the children in Bristol between the ages of five and 13 years was registered at any school.[16] Shocked by these findings, the Board took action to provide more school places and used its discretionary powers to make education compulsory for children up to 13 years old, although, in practice, frequent exemptions were made for the older children. Some of the church schools which could not afford to meet the Board's standards were taken over but both St Andrew's and St Barnabas's remained outside the state sector.

Towards the end of the century it was becoming apparent that another school would be needed to meet the needs of Montpelier's increased population. A site was found in Fairfield Road for what would be Montpelier's only secular Board School. The vicars of St Andrew's, St Barnabas's and St Bartholomew's churches opposed the proposal, as did a group of local residents who claimed it would lower the value of neighbouring houses. It was planned as a higher grade school, with infant, junior and senior departments, which would teach to a level beyond elementary standard from a curriculum that included science. However, the Board then discovered it was only empowered to provide elementary education and had to await legislation that would set up LEAs with the necessary powers. So, although Fairfield Road School was opened in 1898, it was only recognised officially as a secondary school in 1905. From that date scientific and commercial subjects became part of the curriculum and pupils could stay at the school until the age of 16 or 17 years.

Fairfield Higher Grade School, as it became known, was designed by William Larkin Bernard, architect to the School Board, and built by Stephens, Bastow of Bath Buildings at a cost of £25,000. Within an hour of its opening, on 3 November 1898, all 1,054 places were filled and a further 300 children had to be refused admission.[17] The fees were 5d. per week, reduced to 2d. for infants, with 25 per cent of the places free, allocated by competitive examination.

Colston Girls School

A few years earlier another school had opened in Montpelier. Colston Girls' Day School was funded by the Edward Colston Trust, administered by the Society of Merchant Venturers, and governed by a committee consisting mainly of Merchant Venturers and their wives. The site for the school was chosen because it was 'surrounded by villas of a class likely to provide girls for the school'[18] and was close to the newly developing suburb of St Andrew's, which was also thought likely to be a suitable catchment area. The site was easily accessible by road, tram and railway and would therefore attract pupils from other parts of Bristol.

The land cost £2,700 and expenditure on the building was estimated at around £10,000. The ubiquitous Stephens, Bastow won the building contract and William Venn Gough was appointed as architect. Its style has been described by the kinder architectural historians as 'confused'; the best that Andor Gomme can find to say about it is that 'it has a gaudy cheerfulness'.[19]

The school opened on 18 January 1891, with 202 pupils, but it was not long before all 300 of its places were filled. As predicted, many of the girls came from the residential districts closest to the school but some travelled across the city. The school was open to 'all girls who are of good character and of sufficient bodily health'.[20] There was no entrance examination. Fees were £5 per annum, with 10 per cent of places free; pupils were expected to buy their own books. The curriculum included Natural Science, French and Swedish Drill; Latin was optional. The availability of tuition in Latin, then compulsory for university entrance, and the emphasis on preparation for external examinations was an indication that an academic education was offered to those who might benefit from it. A drop in the number of applicants to the school in 1898 was thought to be due to the opening of the co-educational Fairfield Road School, but the effect was short-lived for by the following year applications had returned to their normal level.

The Churches

When St Andrew's Church was being planned a piece of land alongside it was reserved for a Vicarage. Probably because of a shortage of money, this was not built until 1862, almost 18 years after the church itself. When it was finished the vicar must have thought it had been worth waiting for. Designed by the architects, S.B. Gabriel and J.A. Clarke, it was a handsome stone-built house with six bedrooms, a dressing room and light, spacious living rooms. It is still there, although now sub-divided. By the 1870s the church, which had been planned to seat 800 people, was proving too small for its congregation so it was decided to lengthen the chancel and, at the same time, install new vestries and an organ chamber. The extensions, which had cost over £1,100, were consecrated on 11 October 1878.

39 *The hotel sign shows, not inappropriately, a French train.*

In 1882 a Church Extension Commission recommended that new churches should be built in six of the most rapidly growing parishes in the diocese. St Andrew's, which by this time had a population estimated to be 8,340, was one of them. This decision, or, more accurately, the way it was implemented, was to cause the Church Commissioners some embarrassment.

They offered the vicar of St Andrew's £1,000 with the condition that it must be spent immediately on building a church, dedicated to St Martin, in the northern part of his parish. The vicar demurred, suggesting that he put the money on deposit until sufficient funds were raised to guarantee that the building, once begun, would be completed. The response was that he must either use the money at once or else lose it. Foundations were dug on a site at the corner of Chesterfield Road and Sommerville Road in the St Andrew's Estate then, when the walls had been built to a height of four feet, the money ran out. Some years later another site was chosen, money was raised and work started on a replacement church, St Bartholomew's, using the stones from the aborted St Martin's. After its site was disposed of the Commissioners admitted that the whole unfortunate venture had cost more than £10,000.[21]

40   *Fairfield Higher Grade School opened on 3 November 1898 with 1,054 pupils.*

St Barnabas's, with an estimated population of 10,232, was also judged to be an overcrowded parish. Its division seems to have been comparatively painless and the new church of St Agnes was consecrated in 1886. This smooth transition may have been partly due to the fact that Clifton College paid half the cost of the church. Some years earlier they had set up a locally based mission, a socio-religious enterprise that aimed to help needy communities by promoting social and educational activities.

A curate at St Barnabas's, Hardwicke Drummond Rawnsley, was appointed to run the mission but this Oxford-educated, sonnet-writing young man struggled to control the rowdy, disruptive youths in his charge, commenting ruefully that he had to be 'half parson, half policeman'.[22] His tenure was short. After his dismissal in 1877 he left the parish, and Bristol, forever, but not before recording his more pleasant memories of the area in his sonnet 'A Calm Evening on Ashley Hill'. Eventually he found a more congenial post in the Lake District where he went on to become one of the founders of the National Trust.

St Barnabas's Church seems to have had a history of troublesome clergy. In 1860 a local newspaper reported, 'the parishes of St Paul and St Barnabas are again in a state of much excitement, in consequence of the alleged R.C. practices of Mr Liddell, the incumbent, and his curates'.[23] These 'Romish' practices obviously continued for, in 1879, another curate at St Barnabas's was accused of membership of the Catholic Society, as was the curate of St Andrew's, Montpelier.[24] This acute sensitivity to anything connected with Roman Catholicism was a reaction to the rise of the High Church movement within the Church of England. Controversy erupted when, in 1845, the movement's leader, John Henry Newman, converted to Rome because he had doubts about the legitimacy of Anglican claims to continuity with the Catholic tradition. It surged again in 1850 with the re-establishment of the Roman Catholic hierarchy in England which, for Bristol, meant the installation of a Bishop of Clifton, and then again in 1879 when Newman accepted his Cardinal's hat from the Pope. At parish level some Anglican clergy were shifting the emphasis from the Prayer Book to the regular celebration of the eucharist in pre-Reformation form, with vestments, candles and incense. Those who saw these events as proof of the Anglican church's slide towards Rome, and believed it their duty to identify possible deviants, ensured that the controversy continued, at varying degrees of intensity, for the rest of the 19th century.

Monasticism in Montpelier

Montpelier had direct experience of a branch of Anglo-Catholicism when, for a few years, it became the centre for a rather bizarre experiment. Some within the movement were intent on reviving the monastic tradition in England and foremost among them was a Church of England deacon named Lyne. He took to wearing a monk's habit, adopted the name Father Ignatius, and began his mission to refound the Benedictine order in England. In 1863, after he had visited Bristol, a group of his followers gathered first in a house in Trinity Street, then in Trenchard Street, and set up their own cell under a prior called Brother Cyprian. They soon became locally notorious for their 'eccentric proceedings'.[25] These included processing along St Michael's Hill at 2 a.m. on feast days of the Virgin Mary, carrying banners and candles and singing hymns prior to assembling in St Michael's churchyard to hold their vigil. Hostile crowds would gather to taunt the worshippers, and on one occasion violence broke out and police had to break up the procession. In another incident, the police had to be called when two intoxicated brethren attempted to take part in one of Brother Cyprian's services. Father Ignatius ordered the miscreants to do penance in the oratory wearing white sheets, and when they refused he excommunicated them 'amidst great uproar'.[26] After several more of these rowdy events Father Ignatius tried to depose his prior, but Brother Cyprian refused to accept his authority over him and went off with his supporters to start a new monastic order.

In 1866 he took over Montpelier Court, a house in Richmond Road, Montpelier, which has since been demolished. He built an iron chapel in the garden and set up what he called the Augustine Brotherhood. The house became a home for poor boys, run on monastic lines, where they were taught a trade. Some of them were trained as printers and produced religious tracts and a short-lived newspaper called the 'Bristol Daily Telegraph'. On one occasion they were visited by a 'roving bishop', the self-styled Mar Julius, Bishop of Iona, who celebrated the Orthodox liturgy, which he had translated into English, in their chapel.[27]

According to Latimer, the services at the chapel attracted 'a great number of profligate young people of both sexes' and there were many 'unedifying scenes'.[28] In 1872 Brother Cyprian closed his foundation and gave the iron church, dedicated to St Augustine, to the vicar of Bedminster, who erected it at Ashton Gate as a chapel of ease. It was removed from there in 1883 when St Francis's Church was built on the site.

Brother Cyprian, otherwise Charles Amesbury Whitley Deans Dundas, had an interesting background. He was the son of an MP, the grandson of Lord Amesbury, and a member of the ancient landowning family of the Marquesses of Zetland. The setting up of his Montpelier venture coincided with his 21st birthday, when he inherited some family lands which may have provided him with the funds he needed. After he left Montpelier he became a Roman Catholic. He also attempted to enter local politics but was defeated at his first, and only, attempt. Charles Dundas's short but eventful life ended in 1874 when he died of consumption, in Clifton, aged 28.

Other Denominations

On Sunday 30 October 1881 the *Western Daily Press* organised a census in 198 places of worship in Bristol to ascertain how many people attended the services. It showed that, out of a total of 109,452 attenders, 45,518 were Anglicans. St Andrew's two services, one morning, one evening, attracted 643 adults and 100 children. St Barnabas's, with three services, had 723 worshippers.[29] The rest of the church-goers were spread over a range of denominations but the Congregationalists had the largest number. They were particularly well represented in Montpelier and its immediate neighbourhood. There was the long established chapel in Brunswick Square and the more recent building in Arley Hill, but they also worshipped at the Whitfield Memorial Chapel at 85 Ashley Road and at the City Mission Chapel near the bottom of York Road, where there was seating for 150 people. Then, in 1881, they opened the David Thomas Memorial Chapel for their members in St Andrew's and Bishopston. Not far behind them in attendance figures came the Salvation Army, who at that time occupied the Circus, a large wooden structure originally built for visiting circuses in Backfields, behind Stokes Croft. In 1896 they moved into a purpose-built Citadel in Ashley Road. The popularity of their services was probably not unconnected with the crowd-drawing actions of their officers who would walk backwards along Stokes Croft, waving their umbrellas in the air while singing 'We're travelling home to heaven above'.[30] Baptists in Montpelier could attend the chapel in City Road which had opened in 1861. Then, in 1879, they obtained their own, much smaller, chapel, which was built in Albany Road. It was later sold to the Primitive Methodists who, in 1891, built their Sunday School next door.

Recreation

One of the drawbacks of Montpelier's piecemeal development was that no provision was ever made for any permanent, usable open space. In contrast to the planned 18th-century building schemes, which had included communal gardens in the overall design of the squares and terraces in the new urban areas, in the next century population pressure and the desire for a quick profit meant that public green spaces became an unaffordable luxury. Rennison's Pleasure Gardens, Montpelier's greatest asset, had been lost and recent house building had gradually encroached on the spaces the Georgians had left. The other major erosion of green space occurred when land which had been thought to be inviolable was requisitioned for the building of the railway.

This loss could, to a certain extent, be offset as long as there was easy access to the fields north of St Andrew's Road where children could play within reasonable distance of home. This is borne out in the reminiscences of some of those who grew up in the area during the 1870s and '80s. There was 'the long stretch of fields from St Andrew's Church to Ashley Down, happy hunting ground for wild violets, primroses and cowslips'. Many happy hours were spent kite flying in the fields when 'there were no houses between Cromwell Road and Muller's Orphanages'.[31] However, once the plans for the building of the St Andrew's Estate were submitted for approval it became obvious that the fields which had been the children's playground would soon disappear under houses.

Hopes were raised that some compromise was possible when, in 1883, James Derham, the owner of the land, offered to sell 16½ acres to the City Council so that they could preserve it as open space. Unlike the newer industrial cities, which financed the provision of public parks and recreational amenities, Bristol adopted a more passive attitude, relying on landowners to donate or sell to them a piece of land that they could then lay out as a public park, although any land offered for purchase had to be cheap.

41   *Colston Girls' School opened on 18 January 1891 with 202 pupils.*

The price that Mr Derham was asking for his 16½ acres, £12,400, was judged to be too high so the City Council rejected his offer. During the next few years local children continued to play on the land until, when its loss to new building appeared imminent, a meeting of local ratepayers forcefully put the case for saving it to the City Council representatives. Starting from the premise that all building land was expensive, they argued that there was no reason why this densely populated and rapidly growing part of the city should not have 'a share in the advantages enjoyed by other districts in the matter of open spaces'.[32] The City Council agreed to reopen negotiations with Mr Derham to purchase a smaller area of land. Finally, in 1890, they offered, and Mr Derham accepted, £6,600 for 10 acres, 3 roods and 39 perches which they would convert to a public pleasure ground. They and the owner would share the cost of making the roads bounding the park.

Once the land, which had been used for quarrying, had been filled it was divided into two levels, one of which was designed as 'an ornamental pleasure ground' and the other as a children's playground. A drinking fountain and a bandstand were erected and plans were made for three band concerts a week.[33] St Andrew's Park was formally opened on 1 May 1895. It had cost a total of £8,500.

Swimming

As the history of Rennison's Baths shows (see Chapter 6), Montpelier was well ahead of the rest of Bristol in the provision of bathing facilities. Not only was Rennison's older than any other pool in the city, it also had a history of continuous use since the middle of the 18th century. There were two other private baths, in Clifton and Kingsdown, but they were built much later, and the City Council did not open a purpose-built swimming bath until 1884. This was the year in which the Committee to Inquire into the Condition of the Bristol Poor stated that Rennison's Baths were widely used and recommended that the Corporation should own more baths, some of them open-air, for which Rennison's might be a fit model. The extent to which they were used is reflected in the length of their opening hours: 6 a.m. to 8 or 9 p.m. every day in summer. The admission charge was 1d., with another 1d. for the hire of a towel; the attendant's wage was £1 per week.

In the Baths' Committee Minute Book of 1903 there is a reference to the need to provide 'a competitors' waiting room', an indication that swimming at Rennison's had become a competitive sport as well as a recreational pastime. The drawbacks of open-air bathing were highlighted in a letter, sent by the Town Clerk to the Station Master at Montpelier in 1897, complaining about 'the nuisance caused by the beating of carpets on the railway embankment overlooking the Baths' and requesting him 'to stop the practice of throwing stones from the Embankment into the Baths'.[34]

The advertising of winter skating at the Baths (see p.42) may signify that by 1897 this too had become an organised, possibly commercial, event which brought in revenue for the Corporation.

Cycling

In *The Cyclist* magazine published throughout 1886 there is a reference to a thriving Montpelier Cycling Club and also to the existence of training grounds for cyclists.[35] No other information about this club has come to light but there was a local facility which may have been the one used by the club members. The evidence for the existence of this ground is provided in the Ordnance Survey map of 1881, which shows an area of land between

Cheltenham Lane and Station Road marked Bicycle Ground. The site is also referred to in the deed that conveyed the land for the building of Colston Girls' School, described as a Bicycle Works with its entrance in Cheltenham Lane.

In the 1870s and '80s cycle racing was attracting a large popular following. The Bristol Tricycle and Bicycle Club, which was formed in 1876, drew a crowd of 10,000 at its first meet. Serious cyclists needed training grounds and the land in Station Road, close to the railway station and with a bicycle factory on hand, may have proved very suitable. It may also have been used by ordinary cyclists who wanted to learn to ride away from the curious gaze of their neighbours. 'Cycles for hire and riding taught' was an advertising sign frequently seen around this time. Although there is no proof that the proprietor of this particular bicycle factory was running such a business it does seem quite likely.

Public Houses

Nineteenth-century public houses had functions that extended well beyond that of serving liquor to patrons in convivial surroundings. People went there to play games, and billiards was especially popular during this period. The *Old England* was the venue for local cricketers, who practised in the nets behind the tavern. One landlord would have pleased his regular patrons, and possibly brought in some new ones, when he advertised in the *Bristol Magpie* in 1889: 'Important to all interested in cricket Gloucestershire out-matches. The Landlord has arranged to have the result of each day's play wired on drawing stumps'.[36] His enthusiasm would have been shared by two later landlords, who had played professionally for Gloucestershire: wicket-keeper Jack Board and fast bowler Fred Robertson. By 1891 the *Old England* had become the centre for a different game. In that year the *Bristol Magpie* reported, 'The ancient and manly game of Quoits is reviving in Bristol North. Some splendid play can be seen adjoining the Old England Hotel'.[37]

The larger public houses were often used for public and private meetings, dinners, auctions and even inquests. The *Bristol Mirror* of 3 October 1863 carried an account of an inquest into what was obviously a tragic local suicide. Since *felo de se* (wilful self-murder) was at that time a criminal offence which brought shame on the family of the deceased person, verdicts were often quite tactfully worded:

> An Inquest was held last Tuesday at the Old England Tavern, Baptist Mills [*sic*] on the body of Charles Clinch Martin aged 20. He expired at his father's house, Field Villa, Richmond Road. The unfortunate young man had been suffering from consumption and his mind had become affected. Verdict: Death by consumption.

42 *St Andrew's Vicarage, a handsome stone-built house of 1862.*

Libraries

The Public Libraries Act of 1850 authorised local authorities in large towns to provide free public libraries but Bristol was slow to implement the new legislation, mainly because of its financial implications. The Montpelier area did not get its own branch library until 1901. Meanwhile, residents could use the old City Library in King Street, which, dating from 1613, was one of the oldest municipal libraries in the country; then, from 1877, the North District Library which served the wards of St James and St Paul and occupied premises in King Square. Its popularity can be gauged from tables for the year ending 1889 which showed that over 74,000 books had been borrowed and that the magazine and newsroom, open daily from 9 a.m. to 10 p.m., had been used by 202,700 people.[38]

In 1898 it was decided that this usage justified the provision of a larger, purpose-built library in a place closer to the more populated areas. A site in

Cheltenham Road was acquired and an architect, William Venn Gough, who had designed Colston Girls' School, was appointed. The result was an impressive three-storey brick and stone building (only fragments remain after wartime bombing) which cost a total of £11,400. It opened to the public in February 1901 as the new North District Library. From the start it was well used, with the number of readers far exceeding those who had visited the old library.

The Floods

In the low-lying districts of Bristol the final decades of the 19th century were dominated by two major floods and their aftermath. In October 1882 constant rain followed by exceptionally high tides caused the River Frome to rise 15 feet above its normal level. All the streets around Sussex Place were several feet under water and those who were trapped in their houses could only be reached by raft or boat. A baker on his delivery round was drowned in Mina Road and the vicar of St Barnabas's waded through the flood to rescue a blind man from his cottage and carry him to safety on his back. More than 160 houses in Baptist Mills were condemned as unfit for habitation because of irreparable flood damage. The floods of 1889 caused even greater devastation. In early March snowstorms were followed by a rapid thaw and 48 hours of rain. This produced the worst flooding in living memory which, this time, was not confined to the low-lying areas in the suburbs but extended into the heart of the city.

The reasons why these floods were so much more widespread and destructive than any known previously were all too visible. The streets of densely packed houses, built in haste and often with poor materials, that had sprung up during the past few years were both the cause and the first victims of the flooding. They had been built on fields which, formerly, in times of heavy rainfall had served as natural reservoirs for the River Frome. Now, when the rain fell, it bounced off the hard, smooth surfaces of roofs, roads and pavements and had nowhere to go other than into the already swollen, overflowing river.

The same process, but on a smaller scale, was being repeated on the banks of one of the Frome's tributaries, the Cutler's Mill Brook. In Lower Montpelier by the 1870s all the best building land had been taken. The early developers, who had the luxury of choice, had prudently avoided building on the meadows adjacent to the brook. Their late 19th-century successors, left to balance profit against risk, took the predictable decision. Putting their faith in the existing drainage system, they built quickly and intensively along the length of the brook. The *Bristol Times and Mirror* described the state of the building site in 1889:

Within the past twelve months or so, the whole of the field between Banner Road and Cheltenham Place, Montpelier has been raised more or less by house refuse and other material, and the brook, which used to run open along the back walls of the houses in Banner Road, has been covered over, and about 200 houses have been rapidly put up on the field, the road through which is called Shaftesbury Avenue.[39]

What was discovered later was that the covering over of the brook had been done by the owner of each house that abutted it 'according to his fancy, the series of widths and heights quite independent of each other'.[40] This amateur culverting was tested by the storms of 8/9 March 1889. The *Bristol Times and Mirror* reported the outcome:

The flood water, unable to enter the narrow culvert, rushed at great speed along the roadway like a mill stream, sweeping down the walls of numerous villas. Some of the residences are in the course of erection, and much building material lying about broke up the swiftly rushing stream into a number of eddies, the effect being that of flow of a shallow river dotted with large boulders.[41]

Garden walls were swept away and basement and ground-floor rooms in Albany Road, Brook Road, Lower Cheltenham Place and Sussex Place were under a considerable depth of water. The *Bristol Observer* of 16 March 1889 concentrated on the poignant domestic details: 'In a house in Sussex Place a piano floated in the hall and chairs were washed through the kitchen window into the back garden.'

This type of graphic press coverage, coupled with vociferous criticism for their having failed to implement the preventive measures recommended by the City Engineer after the 1882 floods and possible fears of compensation claims from city businesses, jolted the City Council out of its customary complacency. Members were still reluctant, however, to commit the £200,000 needed to provide the real solution to the drainage problem: a gigantic conduit for the River Frome from Stapleton Road to the Avon at Black Rock, tapping in its course the Cutler's Mill Brook. Instead they opted for piecemeal schemes which included relief culverts for both the Cutler's Mill Brook and the Boiling Wells Brook, estimated to cost a total of £46,000.

While the councillors were deliberating, Cutler's Mill Brook overflowed again, in November 1894, causing considerable damage in and near Picton Street and flooding in Mina Road. Two years later the City Engineer reported that the brook's condition was even worse than in 1894. From Bath Buildings to Mina Road it was 'more or less obstructed with stones, bricks, rubble and detritus'.[42] It was calculated that 500-600 loads would have to be removed at a cost of £400. After receiving this report the City Council seemed to be on the brink of implementing the scheme for the relief culverts but, when it was put to a vote, the majority rejected it. It took another spate of flooding to change councillors' minds and to propel them into making an application to Parliament for power to construct the culverts. This was granted in the Floods Prevention Act of 1899.

The Cutler's Mill relief culvert took the streams from Horfield and Westbury which, until then, had flowed into four separate culverts and united them in a seven-ft high culvert. This ran in an almost straight line from the railway arches in Cheltenham Road to discharge its waters into the Frome. The route taken went behind Colston Girls' School, under the gardens of some houses in Bath Buildings and Cheltenham Road, across the top of Picton Lane and Ashley Road, then through St Paul's to the Frome at Broad Weir. The Floods Committee approved the payment of £3 to the owner of 150 Cheltenham Road for the right to construct the culvert under the property.[43] There is no record of any other compensation payments.

The Boiling Wells relief culvert was laid from the point where the stream crossed the South Wales Union Railway, passing under both railway embankments to reach Mina Road. From there it ran across the park to rejoin the old course of the brook and discharge into the Frome at Botany Bay. Both culverts were completed in 1902.

Ten

THE TWENTIETH CENTURY
1900-1939

The scramble for building land in the latter part of the 19th century had left little scope for physical changes in Montpelier's townscape during the next century. In the immediate future any additional living accommodation was more likely to be provided by sub-dividing existing houses rather than by building new ones. A few shops and public houses were modernised around the turn of the century but none as radically as the *Berkeley Castle* in Cheltenham Road. The complete rebuilding of this inn around 1900 made a distinctive contribution to the local street scene. It was built in the style of the Arts and Crafts Movement by the architect Edward Gabriel, who was regarded as one of the best local exponents of the style. Only the upper storey remains today, the ground-floor frontage having been completely altered. Some roads were widened to cope with the increasing amount of traffic. In 1910 the *Old England* gave up a piece of its land and the *Prince of Wales* its forecourt for the widening of Bath Buildings. At the junction with Cheltenham Road a few houses and a shop were demolished around 1930 for the realignment of the road. Then, in 1932, part of Ashley Road was doubled in width. Since all these changes occurred on the periphery of the area its internal layout remained undisturbed.

Housing

Some of the larger houses in Ashley Road had already been converted to institutional use before the end of the 19th century: number 87 had become a Lock Hospital and number 89 a Salvation Army home for women. When the hospital closed in 1924 it was replaced by the Unity Home for elderly people of both sexes. This shift to institutional use was a clear sign that some of the more affluent owner-occupiers were moving away from Lower Montpelier and discovering that their large family homes were difficult to sell. In Montpelier, as elsewhere, most people rented their homes: in the early 20th century 90 per cent of all the houses in the country were rented from private landlords.[1] As

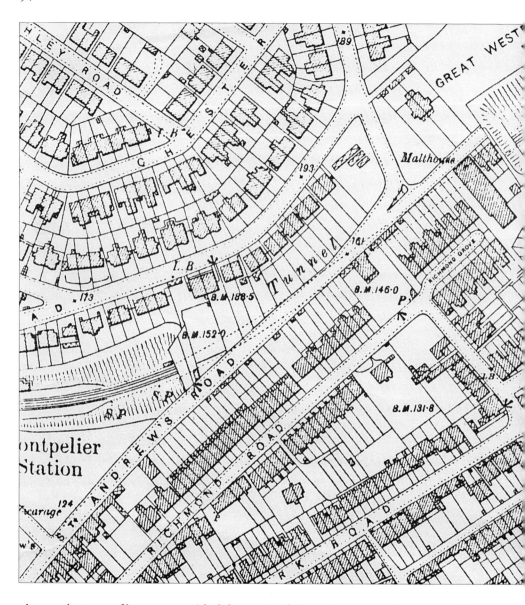

always, the type of houses provided determined the socio-economic composition of an area. There was, for instance, a minor, but important social distinction between parlour and non-parlour houses. All the houses built in Montpelier during the 1880s and '90s, considered very desirable because they had a parlour, would command relatively high rents that could only be afforded by skilled workers in regular employment.

This movement of higher income families away from the area and those with moderate but reliable incomes into it set the pattern for the early decades of the 20th century.

43   *Ordnance Survey map showing Montpelier in 1902.*

Employment and Transport

The first three census returns in the new century reveal a marked increase in the number of Montpelier residents who gave their occupation as 'clerk'. This mirrored the trend in Bristol as a whole, for between 1911 and 1931 the number of clerks in the city rose from 4,625 to 33,308, a consequence of the city's growing importance as a commercial centre.[2] Another 'white collar' occupation that attracted a disproportionate number of local people was that of commercial traveller. It was said that before the First World War 'the area bristled with commercial travellers', and that when they arrived at Montpelier Station on

44   *The* Lord Nelson *public house, now a shop, in the late 1920s.*

Monday mornings extra porters had to be brought in to load their hampers of samples and the personal belongings they needed for the week's travels.[3] Amongst the other regular passengers were those local men employed at Avonmouth Dock. They would catch the early morning train, paying the special workman's fare which, in the early 1900s, was 4d. from Montpelier to Avonmouth.

Lighter manual work could be found closer to home in Coates's Jam and Peel factory, between Cheltenham Road and Bath Buildings, then, in the 1920s and '30s, with the chocolate makers Taylor, Dixon and Co. at 9 Richmond Road. Bakers and delivery men were needed by Matthews' Montpelier Bakery, which had been on its site at the bottom of York Road since 1860. They kept three horses and carts in their stables ready to carry out the promise in their 1904 advertisement: 'Families supplied daily in all parts of the City and Suburbs'.[4]

Employment was also available in the retail trade, especially when branches of large boot and shoe suppliers, such as Massinghams and Stead and Simpson's, opened in Stokes Croft. The small family businesses in Picton Street appear to have continued to thrive – shop premises never remained empty for long. Whereas previously the shopkeepers had confined themselves to supplying just daily needs, during the 1920s three hairdressers and three furniture dealers opened there. The hairdressers were probably responding to the demand created by the new women's fashion for short hair. There is no such simple explanation for the furniture shops. Depending on whether they were selling new or second-hand goods, they could be a sign of affluence or the reverse. There seemed to be self-employed tradesmen in almost every street: no one in Montpelier had to look far for a plumber, carpenter, dressmaker or chimney sweep. One of the new local ventures in the 1930s was the setting up of artists' studios in York Road.

Although the number of professional people living in the area was declining there was still a core of medical men in Ashley Road. At least five doctors and two dentists lived there during the 1920s no doubt because the houses were large enough to keep the surgery and living quarters separate. Clergymen and school teachers were well in evidence and the large number of music teachers in Montpelier, and elsewhere, reflected the buoyant demand for their services during this period.

In the previous century it had been the coming of the railway and the trams that had revolutionised people's lives; in the 20th century it would be the advent of the motor car. However, until the mass production of cars started in Britain the price of the hand-built models kept them out of the ordinary person's reach. Trains and trams were the normal means of transport and Montpelier was particularly well served by both. Over 70 trains went through the station each day on the regular service and that number soared during the summer excursion season. This official information bears out the recollections of local people, which might otherwise be dismissed as nostalgic exaggeration: 'We never looked at the timetable because there was bound to be another train along in minutes.'[5] The number of trams that ran along Gloucester Road made that service equally frequent.

As the century progressed the variety of vehicles on the road increased. In the 1920s there were trams, buses, private cars, taxis, motorcycles and bicycles. During the 1930s the number of private cars in Bristol almost doubled, although, by today's standards, it was still very low. This was the time when popular, mass-produced cars, priced at around £100, were becoming affordable. The effect was visible not only on the roads but also in the types of local businesses spawned and the jobs that became available. The newly formed company of Henly's took over the Cater Motor Company, opening a large showroom at Crofton House, at the junction of Bath Buildings and Cheltenham Road.

Every likely looking site in and around Montpelier was earmarked for use as a motor engineer's workshop, a motor cycle dealer's premises or a haulage contractor's yard. The rapid conversion of the fly proprietor's stables in Picton Lane to a motor workshop was a process repeated in many of the lanes and streets in the area. It is open to question how well qualified some of these engineers were.

Not everyone welcomed the arrival of the motor car. As early as 1909 a surveyor reporting on the state of the premises of Perry and Turner's Carriageworks in Stokes Croft stated, 'motor cars have practically ruined the carriage building trade'.[6] By 1912 the firm which had been on that site since 1804, and had provided work for many local people, was declared bankrupt. There must have been many others who were equally badly affected.

There was another innovation that transformed the lives of local people at around this time, the arrival of electricity. Although Bristol was one of the first towns in the country to have its own power station, opened in 1893, by 1931 fewer than half the households in the city were using electric light.[7] The rest were still dependent on gas or, in some cases, on oil lamps and candles. The reason was electricity's high price. It was only after the unit price fell in 1930 that electricity became economically viable for domestic use. Most houses in Montpelier switched to electric lighting during the early 1930s; then, rather later, electricity became available for cooking.

Education

In 1907 St Andrew's School was condemned as unsuitable for modern school work because of its lack of space and conveniences. Its closure meant that Montpelier no longer had a school in the middle of the community. For their elementary education, which is all most of them had, children had to go to St Barnabas's School or to the infant and junior departments of Fairfield School. When, in 1910, the elementary departments of Fairfield School closed, some Montpelier children undertook the longer walk to the newly opened Sefton Park School.

By the end of the 19th century a national system of free and compulsory elementary education for boys and girls had been established, but relatively little attention had been paid to the provision of secondary schooling. In 1918 a new Education Act was passed which attempted to remedy this. The school curriculum was broadened and children could no longer leave school at the age of 13 if they had a job. To select those children who might benefit from more than elementary education, an examination was devised to be taken at the age of eleven. This would determine whether a pupil entered one of Bristol's secondary, later grammar, schools or applied for one of the free places offered

45 *Ashley Hill in the late 1920s. The shops to the right of the church have since been demolished.*

at the city's independent schools. Those children in Montpelier who passed the examination went to either Fairfield or Cotham Secondary School.

There is evidence to show that some bright local boys used this educational ladder to gain entry to the professions. One, the son of a corn dealer in Picton Street, won a scholarship to Trinity College, Oxford in 1937, another became a senior wrangler at Cambridge and others, often from quite modest backgrounds, went into law or teaching.

The children of Montpelier's professional classes, especially the girls, often started their education in one of the small local private schools. One recalled attending Miss Lucy Innes' Day School for Young Ladies at 98 Ashley Road in the 1920s.[8] There, from the age of four, she was given a good grounding in all the basic subjects, which included French. At the age of 11 she was sent to a fee-paying girls' day school in Clifton. Boys from such families usually received the whole of their education at independent schools outside Montpelier.

46   *The first Metropole cinema opened in 1913. Archie Leach (Cary Grant) went there regularly.*

Recreation

Until the early 1900s the only entertainment outside the home consisted of occasional visits to the theatre, the music hall, the touring circuses or the annual fairs. Then came the development of cinematography, which revolutionised the way people spent their leisure time. By the 1930s, far from being a rare treat, a visit to the cinema had, for many, become a regular twice-weekly event. The first moving pictures were shown in Bristol in 1896 but it was not until 1909 that a permanent picture house opened.[9] The next year one was built for the residents in the Montpelier area. Ralph Pringle, founder of the North American Picture Company, bought a site at the bottom of Cromwell Road, demolished the three shops and two houses that stood there and replaced them with a cinema which could seat 1,400. Pringle's Picture Palace was obviously designed to impress; it had a grand circle which was reached by a marble staircase and an adjacent fully furnished lounge where patrons could mingle. In the more stylish cinemas, like this one, the sense of escapism and anticipation was enhanced by the sight of the uniformed commissioner in the foyer and the showy Wurlitzer organ rising from beneath the floor in front of the screen. When a new owner took over he changed the name to the Zetland Picture House and later it became the Scala. It was demolished in 1974.

The next local cinema to open was much less opulent than Pringle's. The Metropole, which was built on the site of Criterion Cottages in Ashley Road, and opened in 1913, was just a basic, functional structure. Then, in 1938, after the arrival of talking pictures, it was replaced by a luxurious, soundly built, modern cinema which could hold 1,460 people. The earlier name was embellished to mark the change, becoming the Metropole de Luxe. Montpelier residents remember the plush seating and the carpeted first-floor tearoom with its glass-topped tables and Lloyd Loom chairs. It closed in 1968. The building became a Bingo Hall then, in 1980, a furniture store before it was pulled down for a block of flats to be built in 1990.

In 1914 a third cinema opened in the area, the Plaza, later the Academy, in Cheltenham Road. Like Pringle's Picture Palace, it was designed by W.H. Watkins, who was then in great demand as a cinema architect. In 1956 the building was sold to the Christadelphian Church for £7,000. In 1999 it underwent

47   *The Metropole de Luxe built in 1938, subsequently became a furniture store.*

48   *Cary Grant, the Hollywood star.*

49   *The house in Picton Street where Cary Grant lived with his father and grandmother.*

a radical change of use when it was converted to a public house. The new owners did, however, revive the cinematic link by naming it *The Magic Box*, the title of a film about William Friese Greene, said to be the inventor of cinematography.

But even these three cinemas were not sufficient to meet local demand. So, between 1922 and 1936, a temporary floor was laid over the pool at Bristol North Baths for the winter months and films were shown to the patrons who sat in the viewing area on the balcony.

Montpelier was not exceptional in having four cinemas within walking distance of most of its residents; other areas were just as well provided for. The public's appetite for this form of entertainment seemed insatiable. In an attempt to meet it 35 cinemas were opened in Bristol between 1908 and 1916, increasing to a total of 61 by 1940.

One of the local youths who frequented these cinemas was Archie Leech, better known as Cary Grant. In 1913, after his mother was committed to the Fishponds Asylum, the nine-year-old Archie and his father went to live with his father's mother at 21 Picton Street. The father and son had the front downstairs room and Archie slept in the back bedroom on the top floor. While living there Archie attended, and was expelled from, Fairfield School. According to one of his many biographers, Archie went regularly with his father to the

Metropole to see the popular thrillers and the slapstick comedies that he particularly enjoyed. He remembered the cinema as 'a barn like building with hard seats and bare floors, where all the men smoked'.[10] On Saturday afternoons Archie went to Pringle's Picture Palace where he could sit on the balcony for 2d. He lived in Picton Street until 1918 when, at the age of 14, he left Bristol to join a theatre company.

Street directories show Archie's grandfather, Samuel Thomas Leech, at that address between 1882 and 1906; then, presumably because he had died, his wife is listed as the householder. There is some confusion about Samuel's precise occupation. The only information he gave about himself was that he was an artist. The writer of a letter to a local newspaper recalled that around the 1880s there was in Picton Street 'a famous scenic artist, F. Leech, whose animal studies were in great demand for the front cloths at the many menageries and circuses which then toured the country'.[11] If the writer had misremembered the artist's initial he could have been referring to Samuel Leech, or F. Leech may have been another of Archie's relatives.

Cary Grant was not the only actor to be closely connected with Picton Street. A bronze plaque (now painted), edged with a laurel wreath and bearing the words 'Sir Henry Irving, Actor, Lived Here', was placed high on the Picton Street wall of number 9 Ashley Road. For most people that name will now have little resonance, but in the 19th century Henry Irving was revered as the greatest actor of his generation. He was born John Henry Brodribb in 1837 in the Somerset village of Keinton Manderville. When he was about five years old his father, Samuel Brodribb, came to Bristol in search of work. He already had strong links with the city: his brother was settled there and he himself had served his apprenticeship as a silk mercer and been admitted as a burgess in 1826. Samuel and his wife moved to Bristol but sent John Henry to live with his aunt in Cornwall on the understanding that he would come to his parents during the school holidays.

Henry Irving's biographers give only sketchy, and sometimes contradictory, accounts of his early years so it is not easy to establish the facts. The progress of his career is very much more clearly documented. His parents may have, quite unwittingly, prepared the way when they took him to live with them after they moved to London around 1848. It was there that his acting talent emerged and was recognised. Despite strong opposition from his mother, who believed acting was an immoral occupation, he launched himself on to the professional stage. His striking appearance and mesmeric acting skills, displayed in tragedy, comedy and melodrama, captivated audiences. He went on to dominate the British stage for almost fifty years, often in partnership with Ellen Terry. He became an immensely influential actor-manager of the Lyceum Theatre in

London, where he engaged the then unknown Bram Stoker as his business manager. Henry Irving was the first actor to be knighted, thus achieving his ambition to make acting a respectable profession and, he may have thought, vindicate his earlier defiance of his mother's wishes.

Information about his connection with the Ashley Road house is fragmentary and, mostly, unreliable. All that is certain is that it was occupied by members of the Brodribb family, possibly intermittently, from 1825 to the late 1870s. There is no proof that it was Henry Irving's home, although if his parents were living in the house at that time he would have spent his school holidays there. He definitely visited regularly, especially after his widowed father moved there to live with his sisters.

Unlike his wife, Samuel Brodribb was extremely proud of his famous son, kept a detailed diary of his theatrical triumphs and 'enjoyed the regard of his neighbours as an authority on theatrical matters'.[12] From their correspondence, published by Henry's grandson, it seems that the relationship between father and son was close and affectionate. Samuel even responded with equanimity when Henry told him he wanted to change his surname legally to Irving. When Samuel died in 1876 his son followed his cortège from Ashley Road to Brunswick Square cemetery, where he was buried. When Henry Irving died in 1905 his cortège passed through the streets of central London, which were packed with silent mourners, on its way to Westminster Abbey, where he was buried in Poets' Corner. 'Flags throughout the kingdom were flown at half mast and the newspapers of the world published columns of eulogy and appreciation.'[13] A statue of him was placed outside the National Gallery.

While the arrival of the cinema provided local people with ample opportunities for indoor entertainment, it coincided with a significant loss of outdoor recreational facilities. The immediate consequence of the closure of Rennison's Baths in 1916 was that Montpelier residents had to walk up Gloucester Road to the Bristol North Baths and the winter skaters had to go elsewhere. It also meant that local groups, like the St Andrew's cub and scout troops, had lost a meeting place. However, the repercussions of this closure, and the subsequent sale of the site, extended far beyond such inconveniences. This was the only sizeable piece of land in Montpelier in public ownership and its loss effectively prevented the future provision of any substantial amenities for the local community.

Two contrasting leisure activities that could be pursued locally around this time would both have a very limited appeal. One was the game of bowls, which could be played on the new green laid in St Andrew's Park in 1915. The other was shooting practice, which was available at a shooting gallery that had been set up, at some indeterminate date, in Picton House. Next door to this was the

North Bristol Boys' Institute, which was built around 1907 on the side garden of Picton House. It is not clear who started this club but it was probably one of the many socio-religious organisations that would provide a programme of 'improving' activities which would keep boys off the streets and fully occupied. The building's façade, in the style of a Nonconformist chapel, and residents' memories of the Bible Study classes and hymn singing that took place there, led to its being known as 'the old chapel'.

There is little evidence of the effects on the Montpelier community of the really momentous events of these decades, such as the 1930s Depression, the General Strike and, above all, the Great War. The

50   *The plaque to Sir Henry Irving.*

economic upheavals had of course much less impact on Bristol than on towns which had a concentration of heavy industries. Once again, the city benefited from the diversity of its economy. Montpelier, too, may have been cushioned by the spread of different employment amongst its residents, which probably kept the area relatively buoyant. Nevertheless, there was a significant level of unemployment in Bristol during the early 1930s which gave rise to marches, demonstrations and welfare appeals of which no one in the city can have been unaware.

The General Strike of 1926 would have affected those local people who worked on the railway or were employed at Avonmouth docks. Both groups of workers came out on strike and stayed out for nine days, which must have caused them great financial hardship. The effect on the general public was diluted by the actions of the estimated 8,000 strike breakers who volunteered to unload the ships and to keep the road traffic moving.

Any conclusions about the Montpelier community's experiences in the Great War must also be based largely on assumptions, which are occasionally supported by casual remarks contained in reports of other events. Steps were being taken to conserve resources when the closure of Rennison's Baths was described as 'a wartime economy measure'. A Picton Street resident wrote,

51   *Henry Irving, the leading actor-manager of the 19th century.*

'Mr Redman, the Picton Street barber, was away at the war and his wife had to run the business'.[14] A number of people alluded to the difficulty of obtaining servants for the larger houses because the men who had done the odd jobs and the gardening were away fighting and the women who did the domestic work were now working in factories. It seems from the, admittedly small, amount of local evidence available that it was the social changes, especially the widening of women's horizons, that were the most memorable legacies of the war.

The military aspect must have impinged directly, and tragically, on many local families, particularly after 1916 when conscription for all men up to the age of 50 was introduced. The number of local men killed cannot be verified because, as far as is known, no war memorial was erected in St Andrew's Church.

While, understandably, there are difficulties in obtaining accurate information at this distance about events that occurred during the First World War, it may not have been very much easier at the time. The public had only one source of information, the newspapers, which were, of course, censored, so the picture that was allowed to emerge was often a grossly distorted one. The position during the Second World War was, on the face of it, very different, mainly because the civilian population was so much more closely involved. During that war 66 per cent of those who died were civilians whereas in the earlier conflict the figure was only five per cent. The blitz brought the war directly into many people's lives and radio and newsreels recorded, broadcast and commented on events as they were happening. Yet, this multiplicity of sources did not mean that the public would, inevitably, be more accurately informed than previously. Indeed, it can be argued that the strictness of the measures taken to control the new media made it even more difficult for people to distinguish between truth and propaganda.

Eleven

WARTIME MONTPELIER
1939-1945

The first months after the outbreak of war in September 1939 were eerily quiet, almost an anti-climax after the fears that had been raised. That breathing space was in fact invaluable for it gave the ill-prepared authorities time to organise their resources. Air-raid wardens and fire-fighters were recruited and first-aid classes set up. Young people in Montpelier were urged to enrol for a class that was held especially for them in Fairfield School. Gas masks, identity cards and ration books were issued and private and public air-raid shelters built.

During that first year the two major inconveniences to the public were probably the bus curfew and the blackout. The former meant there was no public transport after 10 p.m. and the latter, which was rigorously enforced by patrolling street wardens, obliged people to prevent any chink of light coming from their houses. Street lights were switched off, leaving pedestrians to find their way by dimmed torchlight while trying to avoid the motorists who were driving with only masked sidelights. After a number of accidents, white lines were painted down the centre of roads, along kerbstones and around prominent trees and lamp-posts. The Victorian lamp standard at the top of St Andrew's Road was an obvious candidate for this treatment and retained its black and white stripes long after the war had ended.

Bristol had its first major air raid in November 1940 when the city centre and Filton bore the brunt of the attack. The following month St Paul's and Stokes Croft were heavily bombed but Montpelier escaped with nothing worse than an unexploded bomb at the bottom of Picton Street, as a result of which the immediate neighbours were temporarily evacuated. Then, in March and April 1941, waves of bombing not only destroyed much of the surviving city centre but also left a trail of death and destruction in the residential inner suburbs. In Montpelier buildings were hit in Cheltenham Road, Ashley Road, Bath Buildings, Wellington Avenue and York, Richmond and Fairlawn Roads in what were nights of terror for the whole community. Colston Girls' School

52   *The lamp standard in St Andrew's Road with its wartime black and white stripes.*

was attacked twice. In the first raid the school library was destroyed and there was damage to the Cutler's Mill culvert that lay underneath. In the second the main school building was only saved by the prompt fire fighting of some naval cadets who were billeted there. On the opposite side of Cheltenham Road the public library went up in flames. The Montpelier stationmaster's house suffered the same fate, as did the Mission Church in York Road.

This catalogue of destroyed and damaged property fails to convey the reality of the poignant human tragedies that were its legacy. The deeds of one house contain the bleak statement that the owner 'was found dead on 17th March 1941 as a result of war operations at 69 Richmond Road'.[1] A whole family was wiped out when 31 Ashley Road received a direct hit and a resident of Wellington Avenue recalled a neighbour rushing home from Stokes Croft, where he had been fire watching, to find his wife's body in the cellar covered with rubble. The husband never recovered and later 'lost his mind'.[2]

Many people did not believe that the surface air shelters provided by the local authority offered real protection and thought they would be safer underground. The crypt of St Barnabas's Church was regarded as an ideal refuge and a large group of local residents used to gather there each evening with their blankets and thermos flasks. On the night of Good Friday, 11 April 1941 one of the bombs that were raining down on the area hit the church, passing through the roof and the floor to explode in the crypt. It killed 24 people. These fatalities were doubly tragic and ironic for, not only did those people die in the place they believed to be safer than any other, but the crypt that had been built for burials 100 years earlier was at last, and by chance, serving what had been its original purpose. The death toll for Montpelier in 1941 is not known but in that Good Friday raid the number of people who died across the city was 257, with 146 injured. Such figures were not released until long after the event because of strict wartime censorship. The Ministry of Information controlled all news output; newspapers and radio were forbidden to publish anything that might give aid or comfort to the enemy or lower public morale. They could not report

the location of any bombing, the number of casualties or the extent of the damage to buildings. Even weather forecasts were banned. Newsreels, which were thought to be giving an accurate picture of what was happening, were doctored to show only selected positive, cheerful images.

The immediate result of such heavy censorship was that rumours circulated like Chinese whispers, worrying the authorities to the extent that they invited people to sign a pledge to spread no gossip and to report anyone who did. This explains the comment of a Montpelier resident describing the death of a neighbour in an air raid: '… but we were not supposed to talk about it'.[3] The longer term effect has been to make it difficult to assemble a body of accurate factual information about the

53 *The lamp renovated and restored to its Victorian appearance.*

54 *Air Raid Warden sign, common in wartime, now relatively rare.*

period, especially when looking at areas outside the city centre. If incidents are not documented it leads to undue reliance being placed on uncorroborated anecdotal accounts, which can be contradictory and often fail to agree on facts as basic as the dates of events.

By the end of 1941 the most intensive bombing was over; future attacks on Bristol were less concentrated and more sporadic. In May 1945, in Montpelier, as everywhere else, there were street parties to celebrate the end of the war in Europe. As people rejoiced they were all too aware of the physical scars that surrounded them, gaps in the terraces of houses and huge craters in the ground. What they probably did not realise was that some of these bomb sites would remain empty for the next 40 years.

Twelve

DECADES OF PROTEST
1950–2000

A history of Montpelier that ended in the middle of the 20th century might conclude that its problems, notably those of high density and lack of amenity space, were the consequence of its piecemeal haphazard growth. In short, that the area had suffered from a lack of planning. In the second half of that century the converse was the case: most of the new problems it had to face stemmed from an excess of planning. More specifically, it was an excess of planning of a kind that was not acceptable to the local community.

The springboard for this was the national mood that prevailed in the immediate post-war period. The end of the war released a pent-up demand for social change, of a kind that would produce a fairer society. Education and welfare were high on the public's agenda but attention was also focused on improving the built environment which, initially, meant demolishing the slum housing in the city's cramped streets and alleys. Soon 'new' became a synonym for 'better' and anything regarded as shabby or old-fashioned was swept away to be replaced by bright, clean, efficient buildings and spaces. Above all it meant acknowledging the importance of that new symbol of freedom, the private car, by smoothing its path: providing more roads and widening those that already existed. It was the authorities' attempts to implement plans to achieve this objective that were to dominate, and disrupt, the lives of the people of Montpelier, and other inner suburbs, during the following decades.

The 1952 Development Plan
Before this could happen central government required Bristol City Council to draw up a strategic plan for development over a 20-year period, subject to a five-yearly review. In preparation for this they carried out a city-wide survey between July 1949 and September 1950 to discover the physical condition of each area and to identify the scope for future improvements. The picture of Montpelier that emerged was, predictably, one of a place with a high population

density and negligible public or private open space. Its gross population density was 67 persons per acre, compared with Cotham's figure of 41, Bishopston's 34 and Stoke Bishop's seven. Against the standard set in the Development Plan of seven acres of open space for 1,000 of the population, Montpelier, with 5.08 acres, had a deficiency of 104.96 acres. Only Easton and Barton Hill had less amenity space. The Plan acknowledged that, despite the planners' good intentions, 'the intensity of development in the areas of the city most in need of open space precludes the possibility of obtaining an even distribution up to the desired standard within the period of the plan'. Neither would it be possible to meet the demand for allotments within Montpelier because there was no land available.

The only alleviation of the problem was likely to come from a reduction in the local population, predicted to fall by 3,000 over the next 20 years, which would give an improved density of 56 persons to the acre. This was expected to be achieved by a continuation of the trend for movement away from the inner city to estates in the fringe area. The other local trend that was predicted to continue, and to increase, was that of the conversion of large houses into flats.

There was more optimism about shopping facilities in the area. Cheltenham Road had 69 shops, none of which was vacant; it was thought to have benefited from the relocation of city centre businesses out of their bombed premises. Both Gloucester Road and Cheltenham Road would be retained as district shopping centres because of their accessible position on busy traffic routes. A provisional list of the city's buildings of architectural or historic interest had been drawn up in which Montpelier was poorly represented. The only houses listed were in Ashley Road: numbers 2, 5, 85-91 and 123-9. Despite being defined as 'buildings whose preservation is a matter of national interest, whose destruction or alteration should not be undertaken without compelling reason', one of them, number 5 Ashley Road, was demolished in 1963 in the face of well-informed opposition, to be replaced with an industrial shed. The survey showed that Montpelier railway station was still well used around 1950. Each weekday there was an average of 740 passengers for the 71 trains. On the roads there were ominous signs of the problems ahead. Because traffic congestion was most acute in the city centre, priority would be given to completing the Inner Circuit Road, which had been started in 1937. To link this road to the motorway it would be necessary to build a radial road 'of parkway character' but that was unlikely to be done within the 20-year period of the current Development Plan. This was the first hint of a road scheme that would have serious ramifications for the Montpelier community. However, before the impact of that plan could be assessed, another, city-wide, project triggered a major controversy in which Montpelier residents played a leading role.

The Outer Circuit Road and the Parkway Link

By the early 1960s it was becoming clear that earlier predictions had under-estimated the growth in road traffic in Bristol. Between 1950 and 1961 car ownership in the city had doubled and it was expected to increase further. So too were daily car journeys by commuters as new companies established themselves in a city which, with its central area cleared and ripe for office development and its easy access to two motorways, offered very favourable investment opportunities.

It was against this background that an overdue Quinquennial Review of the 1952 Development Plan was produced in 1966. This contained radical new road plans which were designed to remove all, or nearly all, impediments to the free flow of traffic. It envisaged the city centre circled by three roads: the almost complete Inner Circuit Road, a Ring Road near the city boundaries, and, between them, an Outer Circuit Road which would cut a swathe through many of the inner residential suburbs. This was to run from Lower Ashley Road, through Easton, Lawrence Hill, Totterdown and Bedminster, over the Floating Harbour and on through Jacobs Wells, to emerge in a tunnel outlet in Queen's Road. It would then cross Whiteladies Road and St Michael's Hill, run down Cotham Road, splitting Cotham into two parts, and then, continuing through a large intersection at Cheltenham Road, would dissect Montpelier as it completed its course.

Although the plans were widely criticised for their lack of precision, it was obvious that any project on this scale, with its multi-traffic lanes, intersections, bridges, tunnels and cuttings, would require large acquisitions of land and demolition of buildings. A public inquiry was held in 1967 at which the Civic Society and the Bristol Society of Architects advanced highly detailed objections to the plans, pointing out their cost and the effect of the projected destruction of much of the city's 19th-century townscape. The result of the inquiry was not announced until 1970, when it was revealed that the objections had been dismissed and the Review Plan approved by the Minister.

When news leaked out that the City Council was starting to acquire properties on the first stage of the road through Easton and Totterdown, prior to demolition, people in the other affected areas realised that the threat was real and immediate. Local groups that had come together years before to oppose the road proposals were now galvanised into direct action. The Montpelier Residents' Association launched their campaign in a letter to the *Evening Post* pointing out that 'nearly half of Montpelier may be destroyed for roads'.[1] They were soon joined by the St Paul's Action Group, an offshoot of the Housing Group that had been set up in 1968 to save and improve the St Paul's housing stock. They saw their efforts being undermined by this new threat to the

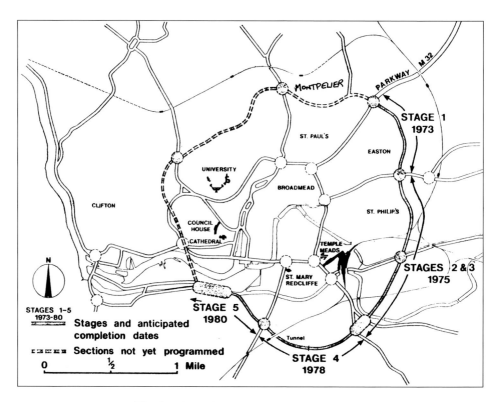

55   *The City Council's proposals for the Outer Circuit Road.*

neighbourhood and united with the Montpelier activists to spearhead local opposition. It was the founder of the St Paul's Group, a Bristol University lecturer named David Hirschmann, who persuaded the disparate bands of people resisting the line of road that would run through their own area that they would be much more effective if they joined forces in a city-wide campaign. It was decided they would function under an umbrella committee, chaired by David Hirschmann, which would co-ordinate activities but would leave each group with its own autonomy. This was a wise move for the campaign was then seen to represent a cross-section of voters, some from less advantaged parts of the city, who could not be dismissed by politicians as middle-class gentrifiers and conservationists.

The political dimension of the campaign was all important because, initially, the protesters needed to convince local councillors that building the road was a folly they would come to regret. In 1971 members of both main political parties on the City Council enthusiastically supported the road scheme. Like their officers, they believed that a good highway network was the key to Bristol's prosperity and, equally importantly, to its prestige.

The campaign co-ordinators immediately started work on researching the factual background to the proposals and devising alternative routes that would be much less socially and environmentally damaging. They enlisted University students to leaflet every household affected by the road, so that residents had the information to enable them to voice their objections to local and national politicians. This led the Conservative leader of the City Council to accuse the students, and their lecturers, of conducting 'a consternation campaign', and his Labour shadow to complain that 'they explained things to little old ladies that will frighten them to death'.[2] *Evening Post* editorials supported the campaign and letters on the subject appeared in the paper almost every day. The joint meetings of the Montpelier and St Paul's residents' groups were well reported and often produced some eye-catching headlines. One declared, 'Millions of pounds should not be spent in wrecking Montpelier',[3] and prominence was given to David Hirschmann's stark analysis of the situation: 'Residents have two choices, either get out of the area quickly while you are still able to sell or stand and fight the plans.'[4] In an interview the City Engineer admitted that the effect on Montpelier was a strong feature of the criticism of the Outer Circuit Road. He went on to offer what he obviously regarded as reassurance to local people : 'The Planning Committee have agreed that the section of the road through Montpelier will not be constructed in its final form within the next 15 years.'[5]

The barrage of publicity and the relentless lobbying of local and national politicians continued throughout 1972. A documentary play was written about the protest and performed at the Theatre Royal. Bristol MP Tony Benn was one of those who saw 'The Bristol Road Show' and strongly recommended it to members of the City Council. By this time the pressure was beginning to affect those councillors who represented the inner suburbs. In November the Labour group, now in power, pledged that the road would not be built beyond Totterdown. They talked about modifying its route but decided to await the outcome of a study they had commissioned into land use and transportation in and around the city (LUTS). By then road policy would be in the hands of Avon County Council, due to take over as highway authority in April 1974. Some Bristol councillors may not have been sorry to relinquish that responsibility.

The campaigners, mindful of the vacillation, intrigue and splits within the political parties, were not inclined to trust mere declarations of intent. They decided to keep up the pressure. The Montpelier and St Paul's groups not only maintained the momentum of their campaign but proceeded to widen its brief. By now plans were well advanced for the Parkway (M32) link to be routed through residential streets in Montpelier and St Paul's. The proposed scheme would channel vehicles via a one-way system from the A38 through City Road and Brigstocke Road and then along Ashley Road to the motorway. It would send a constant stream of heavy, noisy and noxious traffic past the large, multi-occupied Victorian houses in St Paul's that fronted almost directly on to the pavement. In Montpelier it would mean that part of the gardens of the Georgian and Regency houses in Ashley Road would have to be given up for the necessary road widening. In June 1973 the residents' groups canvassed the whole area with a petition demanding that the City Council remove 'the threat of blight from the whole Montpelier area and the immediate threat to use Ashley Road as the main Parkway link'.[6] A fresh strategy was devised. As an alternative to having to conduct what seemed likely to be a perpetual campaign against destructive road schemes, the groups wanted the traffic problem tackled by improving public transport. Montpelier Station had survived the threat of closure during the 1960s Beeching cuts but the service had been drastically reduced. A caption on a newspaper photograph taken around this time describes it as 'a ghost station', left to the weeds and rusting iron.[7] At a public meeting attended by local councillors, residents called for the uprating of Montpelier Station, an improved train timetable and a more efficient bus service that would encourage motorists to use public transport.

After 1 April 1974 the road campaigning groups had to conduct their negotiations with the new Avon County Council. This authority became responsible for highways, transport and strategic planning while Bristol remained in control of local plans and development. As Montpelier residents would soon discover, this two-tier planning system was a recipe for conflict and confusion, but before that the County Council would have to make a decision about the current road schemes. When the LUTS study finally reported in 1975 it recommended that the Outer Circuit Road should not be built beyond Totterdown. It gave as its reasons the road's adverse environmental impact, its low economic benefit and unlikelihood of its ever being cost-effective. The study also favoured abandoning the one-way system for the Parkway link. In 1977 Avon County Council agreed to accept these recommendations. The legacy of these grandiose road plans was a blight that, in some areas, would linger for decades. Irrevocable damage had been done in Easton, where the first section of the Outer Circuit Road had been completed, and in Totterdown, where 550 houses had been demolished to leave a bleak wasteland. Montpelier had remained intact but, during the long period of uncertainty, property values had plummeted, houses had been neglected, and some had been abandoned, then squatted and sometimes vandalised. The journalist Max Barnes, writing in 1973, had urged the authorities to lift the threat of demolition 'that has brought down the standard of the area and hangs like a cloud over everyone'.[8]

The first attempt to lift the cloud was an unmitigated disaster. It was undertaken in the still prevailing belief that an area could be revitalised by sweeping away old buildings. In 1974 Bristol City Council acquired and demolished the terraces of three-and four-storey Victorian houses that stood on the triangle of land between Ashley Road and City Road and replaced them with two large blocks of mainly one-bedroomed flats. The result was described in 'The Fight for Bristol' as 'an affront to the area',[9] a view shared by the Montpelier and St Paul's residents' groups. In addition to being visually offensive the development was also profligately expensive. It was calculated that the building costs worked out at £9,000 per bedroom and to that had to be added the amount paid for the acquisition of the land. City Council representatives later apologised to local people for what they had done: the flats were demolished in 2000.

After this failed exercise in corporate planning and redevelopment the emphasis shifted to finding ways to retain, refurbish and rehabilitate existing properties. It seemed that the speediest way to do that was to take advantage of government legislation that enabled depressed areas to be given special treatment.

The Housing Action Area

In 1975 part of St Paul's was designated a Housing Action Area; then in 1977 this was extended to include Lower Montpelier. The purpose of this project was to achieve, within a five-year period, significant improvements in people's housing and living conditions by offering generous grants and loans for repairs and modernisation. Owners could obtain grants of up to £2,400 for a house and £2,775 for each flat in a house of three or more storeys. This should be set in the context of local house prices in 1977, when a substantial Georgian house in Ashley Road could be bought for £6,000. These grants were only repayable if the property were sold within the next five years. Improvement loans were also available, with repayment spread over 25 years. The City Council would, if necessary, provide temporary accommodation while work was being carried out. If the owners were still unable to renovate their properties the City Council would buy them and carry out the necessary work, often in partnership with a Housing Association.

The Ashley Road houses in Lower Montpelier presented particular problems. Although the one-way Parkway link scheme had been officially abandoned the road widening lines remained. The possibility, and the suspicion, that the highway engineers who had devised the scheme (some of whom had moved to Avon County Council) might still harbour ambitions to make Ashley Road the main route to the motorway continued to have an adverse effect on the marketability of the properties. In addition, many more of the Ashley Road houses had recently been listed as buildings of architectural and historic interest so any repairs or alterations to them would have to be sympathetic and carried out to a high standard, which could make them costly.

Nonetheless, some private owners did take up the grants and loans to restore the houses, while others were acquired by the City Council or the Housing Associations. In 1977 Bristol Churches Housing Association was nominated as the social landlord for the area and within a short time it was buying up large numbers of properties in St Paul's and some in Montpelier.[10]

The Montpelier Conservation Area

The threat of the road schemes did have some beneficial effect on Montpelier. The publicity it generated caused people to take a fresh (or even a first) look at its dramatic townscape and to discover the quality and variety of its buildings. In particular, an article published in the *Evening Post* in the middle of the controversy headed 'Montpelier A Suburb Worth Fighting For' left its readers in no doubt of its value.[11] In December 1976 City Council planning officers began a study of Montpelier with a view to designating it a Conservation Area, i.e. a place of special architectural or historic interest. The study described its distinguishing features: its intact street pattern, the amount of 'charming Regency development' that remained, and Picton Street which, because it had retained so much of the character of a Georgian shopping street, was 'a unique record of Bristol's past'.[12] In addition to the suburb's intrinsic merits, the study pointed to some pragmatic reasons for speedy designation. It would be likely to increase the interest and confidence already being shown in Montpelier's future and would complement the upgrading and revitalisation currently being carried out under the Housing Action programme.

Although Bristol City Council accepted the case for Conservation Area status, there were others who dissented. Avon County Council's planning committee members commented that Montpelier was a borderline case and that further designations such as this would devalue the conservation principle. More specifically, and ominously, they asked that the boundary line be amended to exclude 110-16 Cheltenham Road and 3 Ashley Road, buildings at the junction of the two roads, which would be required for highway improvements. The City Council resisted this request, insisting that the properties were 'an essential group in townscape terms' and that any traffic scheme should be designed around them. The Montpelier Conservation Area was approved in July 1978, with the agreed boundaries of Cheltenham Road, the railway line, Ashley Hill and Ashley Road. The streets around the water meadows were excluded from the designation because they were generally of later date. However, in the midst of these Victorian houses there was a terrace of Georgian artisan homes, numbers 90-124 Lower Cheltenham Place. They had been listed and, it was assumed, given adequate protection. But the assumption was wrong and the houses became the subject of a lengthy and bitter battle between conservationists and Avon County Council.

Lower Cheltenham Place

Around 1970 Bristol City Council began to acquire and to demolish nearby houses in Albany Place and Brook Road to provide a site for St Barnabas's School, which was moving from its City Road premises. Delays, caused by uncertainty about both the Outer Circuit Road and the amount of land that would be needed for the new school, effectively blighted the adjacent property. By 1974, when responsibility for education passed to Avon County Council, the houses in Lower Cheltenham Place were so dilapidated that they were placed on the register of historic buildings at risk. When, in 1977, permission was sought for their demolition, the Department of the Environment refused it. Another application and a public inquiry yielded the same result but, despite this, a few months later some unauthorised partial demolition was carried out. Exchanges between conservationists and the County Council grew increasingly acrimonious. The former accused the Council of acting like unscrupulous property developers in allowing the properties to deteriorate to a point where they could justify the demolition they wanted. The councillors retorted that the houses should never have been listed in the first place.[13]

In an attempt to resolve the impasse Bristol City Council proposed that the terrace be brought within the Conservation Area to make it eligible for special grant aid. Despite strong opposition from Avon County Council the extension went ahead. This did not resolve the problem because the owners refused to take up the grants. Instead the houses lay derelict until 1988 when new owners, in partnership with the City Council and with some funding from an urban aid scheme, started rebuilding the terrace. After almost 20 wasted years the reconstructed terrace (a rather bland copy of the original) was finally habitable again.

The Full Marks Site (110-16 Cheltenham Road)

The aphorism about those who do not learn from history being destined to repeat it was never more aptly demonstrated than in the next major local dispute. It too centred around neglected buildings and their relationship to local authority road schemes.

The site on the corner of Cheltenham Road and Ashley Road took its name from that of a radical left wing bookshop that traded there in the 1970s and

56   *The 'Full Marks' site at the corner of Cheltenham Road and Ashley Road, blighted by road widening schemes for 30 years.*

'80s. The 0.3 acres contained four shops, with accommodation above, and other buildings on the land behind. During 1972 and 1973 Bristol City Council purchased three of the shops, intending eventually to acquire the rest and then clear the site to widen the junction to increase its traffic capacity. In 1974 the buildings passed to the new Avon County Council. Even though the relevant road projects were officially abandoned in 1977 the County Council went on buying buildings and land so that by 1986 they owned the whole site. Their justification was that they would still need it for what they euphemistically termed 'highway improvements'. Avon's officers' commitment to their road programme was made clear in their strenuous objections to the inclusion of these buildings in the Montpelier Conservation Area. It seemed that they were prepared to ignore the warnings from the new, more conservation-minded, City planners that any future highway changes should be designed around these properties.

Once the shops were empty they were left completely unprotected and allowed (some said encouraged) to deteriorate. They were repeatedly squatted and vandalised; one group opened a café there, under the sign 'Demolition Diner'. Campaigners for the homeless highlighted the scandal of these potentially useful buildings falling into dereliction whilst in public ownership.

Then in 1987 the County Council revealed its new scheme to improve the flow of traffic along Ashley Road. It involved the demolition of the shops, the widening of the junction, with a 'refuge' for pedestrians in the road, a pelican crossing and a development of Housing Association flats on whatever land was left over. There would be more demolition of buildings and road widening at the Sussex Place junction. The outrage of local residents was not mitigated by their belief that this was a vindication of their long-held suspicion that the County Council saw Ashley Road as no more than a route to the motorway. From previous experience they knew that their individual views would carry much more weight if they were co-ordinated and presented on behalf of the whole community.

The year before, Patrick and Tessa Roger Jones, veterans of earlier road campaigns, had formed a new residents' group to improve the environment of those who lived in and around Ashley Road. This group, the Triangle Association, immediately swung into action to inform people of the implications of the new proposals and soon found itself acting as the voice of the community. Members attended Council meetings, assiduously taking notes; lobbied councillors and officers; organised a petition and kept the issue alive in the local press. Support came from William Waldegrave, the area's MP, and from individuals and groups across the city. The Victorian Society was scathing in its criticism of Avon County Council's 'wilful neglect' of the buildings and others castigated the authority for sacrificing the community for the commuters. Members of Avon's planning committee who attended a packed public meeting in St Barnabas's School were left in no doubt of the feelings of local people. As the Triangle Association's chairman, Peter Dlugiewicz, put it, 'we will not have Ashley Road turned into a spur of the M32'.

In January 1988, at a meeting of Avon's Planning and Traffic Committee, councillors voted unanimously to reject the scheme and to install pedestrian traffic lights within the existing junction. They also agreed to work with the local groups, which by now included the newly formed Montpelier Conservation Group, to explore ways to retain and refurbish the buildings.

The story did not end there. Over the next few years three developers came forward in turn to try to develop the site, retaining the original buildings. In each case, for a variety of reasons, negotiations with either the Bristol or Avon authorities broke down. In the meantime the buildings were allowed to deteriorate still further. Then, in 1993, Avon's contractors removed the roof, chimneys and parts of the buildings' façade. This was done unlawfully, without the Conservation Area consent that is necessary for partial demolition, and inevitably put the Avon authority on a collision course with its Bristol counterpart. While the two wrangled the buildings were left roofless for

11 months. All this made the future restoration of the properties, which over the years had cost the public well over £200,000, completely uneconomic.

The end result was that the site was eventually disposed of to a Housing Association which rebuilt the shop frontages and erected housing on the back land. This was completed in 2000. Throughout this period the constant refrain of everyone involved was, 'We must not repeat the experience of Lower Cheltenham Place'; but that was exactly what they had done.

No. 3 Ashley Road

When further, authorised, demolition took place on the Full Marks site in 1994 there was a brief opportunity to examine, and photograph, the interior of a building on the back land. From the outside it was an unprepossessing plain brick structure which looked as though it had an industrial purpose. A glance at the inside soon dispelled that impression. It was a room about ten metres square with a stage at one end. Light poured through the huge, unglazed, lantern in the domed roof. On the ceiling and the deep coving below could be seen the remains of ornate plasterwork. Around the room were supporting columns surmounted by Corinthian capitals, and on the walls were friezes with enriched mouldings. Remnants of wood panelling still clung to a few parts of the lower wall.

This was a place that had been built, or converted, for an unknown purpose and sumptuously fitted out, yet no one knew anything about it. Rumour circulated that it had been an early cinema but no evidence had been produced to support that theory. So far it has only been possible to piece together the information gleaned from street directories. The building stood at the rear of 114 Cheltenham Road and it seems that from around 1923 onwards the entire premises were occupied by firms of motor engineers. After the last one left squatters moved in and it was they who appear to have vandalised the property. A member of the staff of the Full Marks bookshop recalled them carrying off the upholstered seating and stripping out the wainscoting for firewood. He deduced that it must have been a place of entertainment and it may be this that gave rise to the story about the cinema. This could be true but, given the amount of light that flooded in from the roof, it seems unlikely.

The first mention of the address comes in a street directory for 1897 but, since only the names of the occupants are given, it is not helpful. Then, in 1908, Robert Hardy, a professor of music, tuner and repairer, moved in and stayed there until 1916. It could be that he used the building not only as a workshop and for teaching, but also as a small concert hall for music recitals and other entertainment. It may also have been a local music club. All this is supposition for, at this stage, nothing can be verified. Nor does any of this information

57 *The building at the rear of the shops which may have been a small concert hall photographed on the day it was demolished in March 1994.*

provide proof of when and by whom the 'concert hall' was built. It could have been converted from an earlier building by Robert Hardy or it could have been purpose-built by a previous owner. There is even doubt about much later uses. It has been suggested that it was a venue for performances by the Unity Players, an agit-prop theatre company that flourished in the 1930s and '40s, but again proof is lacking. Some reliable information may eventually be produced to solve the mystery that surrounds this intriguing building.

Save the Trees

On the morning of Sunday 10 September 1989 contractors moved on to a site in Station Road to fell a belt of black poplar trees that stood on the embankment behind Coston Girls' School. Residents of houses that overlooked the site quickly raised the alarm and soon people were streaming along Station Road to confront the tree fellers. When they refused to stop their work the crowd of onlookers began to position themselves between the workmen and the trees. The police were called, as were the press and TV stations, and reporters

58 *Local protesters gathered to save the poplar trees in Station Road in 1989. They became known as 'The Poplar Front'.*

arrived in time to witness the confrontation. The police tried to persuade the protesters to move off the site and asked the contractors to promise to stop the felling while negotiations took place but the protesters refused to leave, saying they could not trust any undertaking they were given. The next people to arrive were senior planning officers from Bristol City Council, armed with site plans and copies of committee minutes.

They explained that the developers were implementing the planning consent they had been granted in 1981 to build industrial units on this land, and that the consent had been renewed in 1984. To enable it to be carried out the tree preservation orders on the 26 poplars had been lifted and permission given for them to be felled. The planning officers pointed out that the developers, and their contractors, were acting lawfully and that it was the protesters who were in the weak position. The protesters argued that they knew nothing of this old planning decision and that attitudes to the importance of trees in the urban environment had changed since it was given. These particular trees, planted 80 years ago, had become a valued, and necessary, asset in an area which had so little open space and so much hard landscape. The contractors, tired of the arguments, left the site and the protesters, determined that the trees would never be left unguarded, speedily drew up a rota for a 24-hour vigil. That night 15 people slept beside the poplars under improvised shelters made from the six trees that had been felled and sheets of tarpaulin. This was the beginning of a round-the-clock presence on the site that lasted for 11 days. During that time there were periods of torrential rain and the land, already churned up by lorries and earth movers, turned into a mudbath. The protesters built a wigwam and surrounded it with duckboards; the unwritten rule that wellingtons must be removed before entering was strictly enforced. Dry straw came regularly from the city farm and people from nearby houses provided mattresses and dried out sodden sleeping bags. The Picton Street shopkeepers sent supplies of food and local people brought soup and hot drinks. One of the many well-wishers who waved from the trains leapt on to the platform and raced to the site to press a bottle of whisky into the hands of the protesters: then, without a word, dashed back to the train which had considerately waited for him.

There was no shortage of entertainment to keep spirits high. Actors arrived in their street theatre bus and musicians came with guitars, fiddles and tin whistles. A wood carver set to work creating strange and interesting shapes from remains of the fallen trees. Amidst all this activity two ladies, long-term and greatly respected residents of Montpelier, kept their vigil beside the camp fire, calmly knitting blanket squares for charity. Messages of support and encouragement came from people in and around the city. The Post Office gave the site a postal address and agreed to deliver mail sent to Save The Trees.

None of these things diverted the protesters' minds from the ever-present worry that an attempt might be made to evict them forcibly. As a precaution a telephone tree was drawn up to connect each of the people who had agreed to be called out at any time of the day or night. At the same time some serious political negotiations were going on to try to resolve the deadlocked situation. Montpelier Conservation Group, represented by its secretary, David Lambert, who was also a garden historian, was putting pressure on city councillors, urging them to intervene. It was wryly observed that not one councillor could be found who would admit to having voted for the original planning decision, even though it was recorded that only one had voted against it. The other priority was to keep the story in the media headlines. There was a daily press release, reports and pictures appeared each evening in TV's local news bulletins, and some national papers picked up the story. The correspondence columns of regional newspapers provided a useful forum for debate. All decisions about the conduct of the campaign were taken openly, if necessary by a show of hands, at the site meetings that were held each evening at 6 p.m.

Realising that the protesters were not going to leave the site voluntarily, the developers served an injunction on them to regain possession. It was to be

59   *No. 5 Ashley Road, a Georgian house demolished in 1963.*

heard by a High Court judge in chambers. On the appointed day the protesters packed the room to hear the judge award the injunction to the developers, with costs of £1,500 to be paid by the trespassers. Shocked by the level of the costs, the local community rallied to raise the money. People gave generously to a collection in Picton Street and, as the news spread, contributions flooded in from all parts of the city and beyond. Even more important for the protesters was the change in the attitude of the developers. Due, no doubt, to a degree of political pressure and the adverse publicity they had received, they were prepared to make concessions: they would fell only those trees that were agreed to be dangerous and would redraw their plans to accommodate the others. In the event it was found that the contractors had damaged many of the remaining trees by exposing their roots, but the nine healthy trees were reprieved. For the protesters and their supporters this was a much better outcome than they had expected. They regarded it as a heartening example of what could be achieved through community solidarity and resolute action.

Thirteen

THE CHANGING FACE
OF MONTPELIER

If there were times during the last decades of the 20th century when the residents of Montpelier felt they were living under siege, there were some corresponding benefits. Protracted battles against the authorities undoubtedly kept the area in the public eye, but, probably more important, was the fact that they brought together, even if only temporarily, some quite disparate groups of local people in pursuit of a common aim. This was particularly valuable because it came at a time when the community was in danger of losing its stability. As long-term residents with families were continuing to move out of the area they were, increasingly, being replaced by young, mainly single, people who were less likely to have a settled interest in Montpelier. This pattern of movement was reinforced by the type of housing currently being provided which was, almost exclusively, rented accommodation for single occupiers. Some was in newly built flats, such as those on the Metropole site, and some in converted older properties. Nearly all of these developments were carried out by Housing Associations, in co-operation with the City Council, with the aim of regenerating the area. The only large-scale private investment in housing came in the 1990s when the Malt House and the Oast House in Fairfield Road were converted to residential use.

It was many years before all the buildings lost in wartime bombing were replaced. In an article published in 1980 it was pointed out that the Montpelier Mission in York Road was 'still in ruins'.[1] It was to remain in that state for almost another decade. Another, larger, bomb site in Bath Buildings stayed empty until 1988. There was one example of speedy action: the gap in the early 19th-century terrace in Ashley Road was very speedily earmarked for a church. By 1950 a squat, nondescript building had been inserted in the middle of the row of tall, graceful Regency houses; the juxtaposition could not have been more architecturally incongruous. The designers of most of the local post-war buildings displayed a similar genius for disregarding their context. The

60 *Montpelier Health Centre, built in 1997 on the site of Rennison's Baths.*

replacement for numbers 69 and 71 Richmond Road was another low-rise
construction that was completely unsympathetic to its neighbours, although
that did not prevent it becoming the Daily Sketch House of the Year in 1967
(it was demolished in 2003). Again, the long-awaited development in Bath
Buildings consisted of houses that turned their backs to the street, contrasting
sadly with the lively frontages around them.

At the same time new owners were reclaiming some of the older run-down
properties by carrying our sensitive and painstaking repairs to transform them
into very desirable homes. Small local shops that had been lying empty were
converted to houses or offices. The extent of the changes of use that occurred
in Picton Street was not sufficient to jeopardise its role as the local shopping
street. Its fortunes fluctuated, and many new businessess came and went, but
the shops that sold the staple necessities continued to flourish. The 1980s saw
a dramatic improvement in the appearance of many of the shabbier properties

as their owners began to realise that Picton Street, and the rest of Montpelier, had a future.

One very important landmark was lost during this period. St Andrew's Church, which had been built amidst controversy in 1845, was demolished in similar circumstances in 1969. Even though no services had been held there during the past six years, local people had assumed that the church would eventually be used again, even if for non-ecclesiastical purposes. So when the Church Commissioners decided that they 'had to take it down because it was dangerous'[2] there was considerable surprise and some dismay. It was later revealed that the structure could have been repaired for an estimated £900; with central heating and rewiring the total expenditure required amounted to, at most, £4,200.[3] There may have been other reasons for the decision: the congregation had been dwindling and there were problems associated with the retirement of the blind vicar, Canon Harvard Perkins, who had been the incumbent for 53 years. Nevertheless, local people believed that, given the will, a less drastic solution could have been found.

Once the decision had been taken it was speedily implemented, and that too caused controversy. According to eye-witnesses, the site was left unsupervised for much of the time and people could, and did, carry away metal, lead and church fittings that should have been safeguarded. There were even more recriminations when it was discovered, after the bodies of those buried in the churchyard had been reinterred elsewhere, that no record had been made of the original burials. That, of course, meant that the local association had been lost. It seemed that events were conspiring to wipe St Andrew's Church from Montpelier's history.

The site became a playground and the parish was transferred to the Church of St Bartholomew in Maurice Road.

St Barnabas's, the other Anglican church that served the local community, disappeared relatively quietly. It had been re-opened within a year of its bombing in 1941 but did not survive for much longer. In 1955 it was united with St Paul's, Portland Square, with the latter as the parish church. After the closure of St Paul's Church in 1988 the combined parishes were united with that of St Agnes's Church. Meanwhile, the redundant St Barnabas's, which had been temporarily occupied by the adjacent primary school, was demolished for a community centre to be built on its site.

The primary school was relocated to modern, purpose-built premises in Montpelier. The site for it, and the adjacent play area, had been created by the gradual demolition of houses in Albany Road and Brook Road, which was completed in the 1970s. At around the same time, work was starting on the site of Rennison's Baths in preparation for the building of the Montpelier Health

Centre. Some rudimentary archaeological investigations were carried out at the time but they yielded very little. A piece of an 18th-century slip-ware dish was found in a test bore hole but nothing from the original structures; the only wall tiles and paving that had survived dated from the later period of the baths.[4] The Health Centre that was then built was replaced in 1997 by a larger, more up-to-date, centre on the same site.

There were some significant changes in and around Montpelier Station. Against all expectations, the Severn Beach line survived the Beeching Plan of 1963, which reduced passenger lines by one-fifth and closed one-third of the country's stations. Even so, the service was scaled down and Montpelier Station lost some of its facilities. All the Sunday trains were withdrawn and in 1965, when the lines were closed to goods traffic, the goods yard became redundant. In 1967 the Severn Beach line was again threatened with closure and again reprieved, on the grounds that the workers who depended on it, and who were its main users, would be caused hardship. To safeguard the service the government promised to pay the British Railway Board a social grant towards its cost. Montpelier, too, had to pay a price for this second reprieve. In that year all staff were withdrawn from the station and replaced by conductor-guards on the trains. The line was reduced to a single track and the bridge over the approach road lifted. Then all the buildings on the up (north) platform were removed.[5]

Once the station became unstaffed its appearance was allowed to deteriorate. Local travellers lamented the fact that there was now no-one to tend the neat flower beds and hanging baskets for which the station had been renowned. Since then, although there have been intermittent rumours of its imminent closure, the Severn Beach line has survived.

It is relatively easy to summarise the physical changes that took place in Montpelier during this period but much more difficult to assess the importance of any social shifts that occurred at the same time. They will be more accurately judged in retrospect, particularly after detailed census figures become available. Until then only very tentative conclusions can be drawn from observation and from the limited evidence that can be gathered.

One fact that is indisputable is that the diversity of the local population was enriched by the number of people from different backgrounds and cultures who came to live and work in Montpelier during the second half of the 20th century. Among the first to arrive were some Polish people who had left their country during the war and who afterwards elected to stay in Britain. The growth of their community in and around Montpelier led to their acquiring Arley Chapel from the Congregationalists to have it consecrated as a Catholic Church serving the local Polish residents and those from the wider area. A vibrant Italian community also settled locally, some of whom became closely identified with Montpelier through the shops and restaurants they opened there. But by far the largest group of newcomers came from non-European countries. It is impossible to assess numbers because the only figures extracted from the 1981 census returns that showed ethnic origin were for electoral wards rather than specific neighbourhoods.[6] The only information they yielded suggested that Lower Montpelier had a concentration of people who had been born in the New Commonwealth or Pakistan. It was the variety of cultures and languages, of these and many other countries, encountered when shopping or living there, that made Montpelier the cosmopolitan place it became during this period.

Other people moved either within the area or from outside to buy and rescue those older properties that were being sold so cheaply in the 1970s. Their confidence was vindicated when, between 1986 and 1989, house prices in Montpelier rose faster than in any other part of the city. The new house owners were, generally, salaried professional people who, more often than not, worked in the public sector. The relative modesty of the incomes of those who were buying property there may have been one of the reasons why the area was spared the excesses of gentrification that occurred elsewhere. Very few members of the mainstream professions such as law, accountancy and medicine chose to live in the reviving Montpelier, although architects were well in evidence. So, too, were teachers, social workers and those involved in the creative and performing arts. The increasing popularity of complementary medicine, coupled with a perception of Montpelier as a potentially good catchment area, led a number of therapists to set up practices there. But, alongside the residents who were economically secure, were the many others who were either unemployed or had only casual work and therefore very little disposable income. It seems that this was a period in which the population of Montpelier was possibly more mixed, and certainly more mobile, than it had ever been.

This social diversity was the theme of an article about the area that appeared in a local newspaper in 1988. It was a satirical piece in which the writer, who lived in Montpelier, described it as 'a haven for the fashionable, liberal and otherwise alternative newcomers – Bristol's very own Left Bank'.[7] Then the article went on, more seriously, to show that the place was, in reality, much more mixed than this image might suggest. Those who lived there knew that it was also 'a multi-economic, multi-ethnic village', a communal neighbourhood 'where you'll walk no further than 20 yards without stopping to chat'. Late 20th-century Montpelier is not, the writer observed, 'a conventional area'. But, then, it never was.

Conclusion

It is understandable that anyone who glances at Montpelier and then reads an account of its history might conclude that the congested, built-up inner-city area of today bears little resemblance to the original elegant, spacious, Georgian suburb. Yet a closer look would reveal how little, rather than how much, Montpelier has changed. Admittedly, extra houses have been crammed into every available space, but most of those that were built in the 18th and early 19th centuries are still there. So, too, is the old street pattern of roads that lead up to the fine viewpoint at the top of the hill. Picton Street may have lost some of its original details over the years but it has retained the domestic scale and the visual integrity that make it instantly recognisable as a Georgian shopping street.

Although it is arguable whether many of the more recent buildings have enhanced its appearance, they too are part of Montpelier's history and are evidence of its evolutionary growth. The architectural mishaps that offend some sensibilities may be the price that had to be paid for escaping the deadening homogeneity of the more uniform suburbs.

But it is not only its built environment that gives Montpelier the sense of place that it undoubtedly has, that ambience that makes it unlike any other part of Bristol. While there is general agreement that it exists, this *genius loci* eludes easy definition. One problem is that the area presents so many, often contradictory, faces. It is communal yet cosmopolitan; energising but also relaxing; bewitching yet at the same time exasperating. Maybe it is these paradoxes that are themselves the source of Montpelier's identity. Whatever the explanation, I hope that this study has demonstrated that its unique character has its roots in Montpelier's history and in the lives and personalities of the people who made that history.

Notes

Introduction

1   Smith, A.H., *The Place-Names of Gloucestershire*, English Place-Name Society. Volume XL, Part 3, 'The Lower Severn Valley and The Forest of Dean', Cambridge University Press, 1964.

Chapter 1: The Origins of Montpelier

1   Smith, A.H., *op. cit.*

2   Catalogue of MSS. collected by the Reverend H.J. Ellacombe and the Reverend Samuel Seyer, Bristol Record Office.

3   Samuel Seyer's 'Fragments' contains Brayne family pedigree.

4   Robert Brayne's Will 1596, Probate 11/53, Gloucester Record Office. Ann Winter challenged her brother's will, in which he had made provision for his wife, on the grounds of his insanity. She lost the case and Robert's wife, Goodith, was awarded a life tenancy.

5   A Deed Relating to the Partition of the Property of St James, Bristol. See *Proceedings of the Clifton Antiquarian Club*, 1898, pp. 109-38.

6   Smith, *op. cit.*

7   Bristol Charters 1155-1373: Volume I, Bristol Record Society, 1930.

8   Henry II at an Assize of the Forest in 1184 granted the priory immunity for essarts (wood clearing) on their Ashley Estate. Bristol Record Office P/StJ/HM/4(a).

Chapter 2: The Watermills

1   Smith, *op. cit.*

2   Hook/Hooke, both spellings occur but for consistency I have adopted the latter throughout.

3   Census return contained in Seyer's 'Fragments'. Outparish Rate Book 1651, Bristol Record Office P/StJ/OP/1/1(1 20).

4   *Proceedings of the Bristol Naturalists' Society*, 1897-98, Vol. VIII, part 2, p.174 and Vol. VI, p.317.

5   *The Bristol Oracle*, 8 January 1742.

6   Perambulation of St James's Parish, 1751. Bristol Record Office P/StJ/ChW/6.

7   Aldworth family MSS., Bristol Record Office 09459(3)a-p.

8   Seyer, Samuel, 'Memoirs Historical and Topographical of Bristol and its Neighbourhood', Vol.11 (1823), p.512.

9   Aldworth MSS.
10 Quoted in John Latimer's *The Annals of Bristol in the Eighteenth Century* (1893), p.302.
11 A rack rent is the full value of the property, or as near to it as possible (*Mozely and Whiteley's Law Dictionary* compiled by E.R. Hardy Ivamy, Butterworth's, 1988).

Chapter 3: The Land and Its Owners

1   Deed of Partition, note 1.5 above.
2   Deeds of 19 Ashley Road.
3   Banner's Bristol Journal, 8/1/1785. Quoted in John Latimer's 18th Century Annals, 1893, p.463.
4   Aldworth MSS.
5   Robert Aldworth's Will 1670, Great Orphan Book of Wills, Folio 0.16.0, Bristol Record Office.
6   Deeds of Ashley Place, Bristol Record Office 34901.
7   Bristol Apprentice Book, Bristol Record Office.
8   Humphrey Hooke, son of Andrew, was born in 1661 and matriculated in 1667 at St Edmund Hall, Oxford University. He should not be confused with Humphrey Hooke (1580-1659) who owned the Kingsweston Estate and became infamous for his double dealing during the Civil War. It is likely that the two Humphreys came from collateral branches of the same family.
9   Bristol Burgess Book, Bristol Record Office.
10 Latimer, *The Annals of Bristol*, p.279.
11 Andrew Hooke was following a fashion, started in the London Coffee Houses, of popularising current scientific theories about the nature of the universe.
12 Felix Farley's Journal, 3/2/1753.
13 *Ibid.*, 13/8/1757.
14 Given their reputation for abstaining from alcohol it seems strange that Quakers should engage in such businesses. One explanation is that they were not opposed to drinking, but only to drinking to excess. Another is that the impurity of the water supply at this time made the brewing of light ale essential for health reasons. Crucial is the fact that, as a persecuted sect, Quakers were excluded from the professions and had to make a living in either trade or industry.

Chapter 4: Early Houses

1   Lands in St James, Bristol Record Office 6609(5)
2   Aldworth MSS.
3   Gloucester Inquisitions Post Mortem, Vol.2, British Record Society. Gloucester Record Office.
4   Deeds of Ashley Cottage.
5   The *Building News*, 5/7/1907.
6   Hamilton, H., *The English Brass and Copper Industries before 1800.*
7   Latimer, *The Annals of Bristol.*
8   Pritchard, F.N., *Transactions of the Bristol and Gloucestershire Archaeological Society*, 1908, Vol.XXXl, p.304.
9   Papers relating to Foster's Place, Bristol Record Office 14754(3) and (4)a.
10 Evans, John, 'A Chronological Outline of the History of Bristol and the Stranger's Guide', 1824.
11 Brown, Horatio, 'A Biography of J.A.Symonds Compiled from his Correspondence'.

12 *Bristol Mercury*, 11/6/1842.
13 Salmon, Arthur, *A Book of English Places*, 1934.
14 *Bristol Oracle*, 8/1/1742.
15 Affirmation and Affidavit relative to the rents of Ashley Estate, Bristol Record Office 4964(63).
16 Felix Farley's Journal, 13/6/1776.
17 *Evening Post*, 12/9/1940; 'on Old Ashley Hill', by C. Roy Hudleston.

Chapter 5: The First Civil War
1 Howell, E.B., editor of 'A Complete Collection of State Trials', 1817.
2 Atkyns, Richard, 'Military Memoirs of the Civil War', ed. Peter Young, 1967.
3 Sprigg, Joshua, 'Anglia Rediviva', Oxford, 1854.
4 *Ibid.*
5 *Ibid.*
6 Seyer, Samuel, 'Memoirs Historical and Topographical of Bristol', Vol. II, p.458, Bristol, 1923.
7 Nicholls, J.F. and Taylor, John, 'Bristol Past and Present', Vol. III, p.4, Bristol, 1882.
8 Wigan, Eve, *A History of the Gordano Region of Somerset*, 1950.
9 Deposition Book of Bristol, 1643-47, Bristol Record Society.
10 Latimer, *The Annals of Bristol in the 17th century*.

Chapter 6: Rennison's Baths
1 'The Humble Address of Thomas Renison, Thread Maker of the Parish of St James, Bristol', Bristol Reference Library.
2 Felix Farley's Journal, 22/9/1764.
3 Felix Farley's Journal, 22/6/1782.
4 Latimer, *The Annals of Bristol*.
5 Deeds of Rennison's Baths and Terrett's Mills, the Society of Merchant Venturers.
6 Report to the Health of Towns Commission, 1845.
7 Baths Committee Minute Book 1, Bristol Record Office.
8 *Ibid.*

Chapter 7: The Garden Suburb 1791-1837
1 Title Deeds of Ashley Place, Bristol Record Office 34901(1 8).
2 Mowl, Timothy, *To Build the Second City*, Redcliffe Press, 1991.
3 Latimer, *The Annals of Bristol*.
4 Title Deeds of Ashley Place.
5 Lands at Ashley, Bristol Record Office 6378
6 Deeds of Box Cottage, 16 Fairfield Road.
7 Bristol Record Office 35447, Box 1, Bundle IIIG. I am grateful to Mike Hooper for this information.
8 Deeds of 69/71 Richmond Road and 6 St Andrew's Road.
9 Felix Farley's Journal, 31/7/1813.
10 Felix Farley's Journal, 9/5/1812.
11 Deeds of Apesherd, Bristol Record Office 36888.
12 *Ibid.*
13 City Museum and Art Gallery Ref. M3442.
14 Apesherd Deeds.

15   St Paul's Baptismal Registers 1813-1887, Bristol Record Office.
16   St Paul's Ward Lists, Bristol Record Office.
17   Deeds of Picton House.
18   Hyamson, *Dictionary of English Phrases*.
19   *Bristol Mercury*, 6/4/1830.
20   Bristol Record Office 36014 (1).
21   Deeds of Ashley Place.
22   Undated letter written by Mr Dawbarn, Bristol Record Office 30299(2).
23   Bristol Record Office 6378(28).
24   Auction Notice, Bristol Record Office 35810 WWP/I/10.
25   'Selections from the Reminiscences of Captain Grownow', Aide de Camp to
     General Picton, ed. Nicholas Bentley, Folio Society, 1977.

Chapter 8: Victorian Montpelier – The Early Years, 1837-1860

1   Alford, B.W.E., 'The Economic Development of Bristol in the Nineteenth
     Century', Bristol and Gloucestershire Archaeological Society, 1976.
2   Deeds of 1 Fairlawn Road.
3   Benjamin Maddocks was the proprietor of the garden nurseries at Bath Buildings.
4   Deeds relating to William Williams, Bristol Record Office 4965(25c).
5   Joseph Hemmings, 'Montpelier of 75 years ago', *Evening Post* 12/5/1937, recalled a
     Mr Naish who had a cotton loom working in his garden.
6   Records of the Incorporated Church Building Society, quoted in Ralph and Cobb,
     'New Anglican Churches in c19 Bristol', 1991.
7   St Paul's Vestry Minutes, 1839-1865, Bristol Record Office.
8   *Ibid.*
9   The *Bristol Mirror*, 16/9/1843.
10   Bristol Record Office P/StB/Ch.W/2(a b)
11   Leech, Joseph, *Rural Rides of the Bristol Churchgoer*, 1843-5.
12   St Paul's Vestry Minutes.
13   Felix Farley's Journal, 1/3/1829.
14   St Andrew's School, Bristol Record Office 22938(21).
15   Clark, G.T., 'Report to the General Board of Health', 1850.
16   Health of Towns Commission Report on the State of Bristol, HMSO, 1845.
17   Report on the Preliminary Enquiry into the Sewerage, Drainage and Supply of
     Water and the Sanitary Conditions of the Inhabitants of the City and County of
     Bristol, HMSO, 1850.
18   *The Times*, 18/10/1869.
19   See Harold Nabb, 'The Bristol Gas Light Company', and Building Indexes in
     Bristol Record Office.

Chapter 9: Urbanisation 1860-1900

1   Census figures quoted in C.P. Hill; British Social and Economic History 1700-1964,
     1970.
2   Latimer, *The Annals of Bristol*.
3   Abstract on Title of J. and W. Derham, Bristol Record Office P/StB/Ch.W/4(a).
4   Gomme, Andor, *Bristol, An Architectural History*,1979.
5   'Ports of the Bristol Channel', The London Printing & Engraving Co., 1893.
6   BIAS Journal 13, 1980, contains a plan of the site.
7   See Minutes of the Blue Maids Asylum, Bristol Record Office.

8   Clifton Extension Railway, Deposited Plans, House of Lords Library.

9   Railway Minutes, Clifton Extension Railway.

10   *Western Daily Press*, 2 October 1874.

11   Oakley, Mike, *Bristol Suburban*, Redcliffe Press, 1990.

12   *Ibid.*

13   Bristol Record Office P/StP/V/1, 1845-1945.

14   Street Directories 1870-80.

15   *Bristol Times and Mirror*, 4/11/1870.

16   Gibson, Cyril, 'The Bristol School Board 1871-1903', 1997.

17   Bristol School Board, 10th Report, p. 6, Bristol Record Office.

18   Chairman of the Colston Trust. See Sarah Dunn, *Colston Girls' School The First Hundred Years*, 1991.

19   Gomme, *Bristol, An Architectural History*.

20   Dunn, *Colston Girls' School*.

21   'Horfield Miscellanea An Act of Horfield from Early Times to 1900' by the Rev. Fanshawe Bingham, 1906.

22   Quoted in *Founders of the National Trust* by Graham Murphy, 1987.

23   *Bristol Times* and Felix Farley's Bristol Journal, 14/4/1860.

24   Cobb, Peter, *The Oxford Movement in Nineteenth Century Bristol*, 1988.

25   Latimer, *The Annals of Bristol*.

26   *Bristol Times*, 19/7/1866.

27   *Bristol Daily Post*, 1/10/1866.

28   Latimer, *The Annals of Bristol*.

29   The survey was reprinted as an appendix in Nicholls and Taylor, *Bristol Past and Present, Vol. 2.*

30   *The Salvation Army A Century of Blood and Fire*, Centenary publication, 1980.

31   'More Recollections of Old Montpelier' by Charles F. James, *Evening Post*, 19/5/1937.

32   *Bristol Times and Mirror*, 12/10/1889.

33   Lambert, David, *Historic Public Parks Bristol*, 2000.

34   Minutes of the Baths Committee, March 1897, Bristol Record Office.

35   Harrison, Jo, 'Montpelier 1750-1900', unpublished ms.

36   Quoted in *Bristol's Historic Inns* by Helena Eason, 1982.

37   *Ibid.*

38   Greenwood, T., 'Public Libraries, their organisation, uses and management', 1890.

39   The *Bristol Times and Mirror*, 9/3/1889.

40   City Engineer, 1894-5, Report to Frome Floods Committee, Bristol Record Office 09335 (1-4).

41   *Bristol Times and Mirror* 9/3/1889.

42   Report to Frome Floods Committee.

43   *Ibid.*

Chapter 10: The Twentieth Century 1900-1939

1   Muthesius, Stephan, *The English Terraced House*, 1982.

2   Census returns 1911-1931.

3   Vincent, Mike, *Lines to Avonmouth*, 1979.

4   *The New Bristol Directory*, Sharp and Co., 1904.

5   Interview Ms M. Smith.

6   Bristol Record Office P/StJ/D/16/42/4.

7   See *Electricity in Bristol 1863-1948* by Peter G. Lamb, 1981.
8   Interview Mrs Jessie Moate.
9   See *A City and Its Cinemas* by Charles Anderson, 1983.
10   McCann, Graham, *Cary Grant A Class Apart*, 1996.
11   'More Recollections of Old Montpelier', letter from C.F. James, *Evening Post*, 19/5/1937.
12   Irving, Laurence, *Henry Irving, the Actor and his World*, 1951.
13   *Ibid*.
14   Correspondence with Mr Eric Green.

Chapter 11: 1939-1945
1   Deeds of 69 and 71 Richmond Road.
2   Interview with Mrs Goodridge in 1989.
3   For an account of censorship in the West Country see *West at War* by James Belsey and Helen Reid, 1990, and *Bristol Blitz* by Helen Reid, 1998.

Chapter 12: Decades of Protest 1950-2000
1   *Evening Post* 19/10/1971.
2   Planning Committee Meeting 8 December 1971, reported in *Evening Post*, 9/12/1971.
3   *Evening Post*, 15/10/1971.
4   *Evening Post*, 8/12/1971.
5   *Evening Post*, interview, November 1971, filed in bound copies of Ring Road Schemes, Bristol Reference Library.
6   Parkway Cuttings File, Bristol Reference Library.
7   *Evening Post*, 20/3/1973, in Montpelier File at Cheltenham Road Library.
8   'Montpelier a suburb worth fighting for' by Max Barnes, *Evening Post, 20/3/1973*.
9   See 'The Fight for Bristol', *Urban Renewal*, p.109, edited by Gordon Priest and Pamela Cobb, 1980.
10   St Paul's Housing Action Area: Progress Report, 1977, Bristol Reference Library.
11   *Evening Post*, 20/3/1973.
12   Proposed Designation of Montpelier as a Conservation Area, City of Bristol Planning Department, 15 March 1978.
13   *Evening Post*, 13/5/1982.

Chapter 13: The Changing Face of Montpelier
1   Dawson, David, 'And Bethel Shall Come To Nought', *Avon Past, the Journal of the Avon Archaeological Council and Avon Local History Association*, Issue No. 3, Autumn 1980.
2   *Evening Post*, 15/9/1969.
3   Bristol Record Office P/StAM/P3.
4   Jo Harrison, *op. cit.*
5   See Mike Oakley and Mike Vincent, *op. cit.*
6   *Ethnic Minority Statistics In Avon*, Avon County Council, 1985.
7   'A Halfway House For Would Be Yuppies', *Evening Post*, 11/3/1988.

BIBLIOGRAPHY

Primary Sources: All are in Bristol Record Office, unless otherwise stated:
Ashmead George, *Nineteenth Century Maps*; also in Bristol Reference Library
Bristol Apprentice Book
Bristol Burgess Book
Building Indexes
Census Enumeration Returns; Bristol Reference Library
Development Plan for the City and County of Bristol, April 1952
Guides and Directories; Bristol Reference Library:
    Arrowsmith's Dictionary of Bristol, 1906 edn; J.W. Arrowsmith
    Mathew's Complete Guide and Bristol Directory for 1793-4; Bristol 1794
    Sketchley's Bristol Directory of 1775; Kingsmead Reprints, Bath, 1971
    Kelly's, Sharp's and Wright's Street Directories
Local Government Minutes of Baths' Committee; Baths' and Washhouses
    Committee; Frome Floods Committee; Planning Committee
Newspapers; Bristol Reference Library:
    Bristol Daily Post
    Bristol Mercury
    Bristol Oracle
    Bristol Times and Mirror
    Evening Post
    Felix Farley's Journal
    The Times
    Western Daily Press

Parish Records:
    St Andrew, Montpelier
    St Barnabas
    St James
    St Paul, Portland Square

Reports:
Health of Towns Commission: Report on the state of Bristol; London,
    HMSO, 1845

Report on the Preliminary Enquiry into the Sewerage, Drainage, Supply of Water and the Sanitary Conditions of the Inhabitants of the City and County of Bristol; London, HMSO, 1850;

G.T. Clark, Report to the General Board of Health on above,1850

Title Deeds and Documents:
  Aldworth, MSS
  Apesherd
  Ashley, Chequer Ground
  Ashley Farm and Hooke's Mills, 1720-1863
  Ashley Place
Latimer, J., 'A Deed Relating to the Partitition of the Property of St. James, Bristol'. See *Proceedings of the Clifton Antiquarian Club*, 1898
Pritchard, F.N., 'Ashley Manor House', *Transactions of the Bristol and Gloucestershire Archeological Society*, 1908, Vol.XXXI, p.304
MSS collected by the Reverend Samuel Seyer

Title Deeds privately held:
  Ashley Cottage, 77 Ashley Road
  Ashley Green
  19 Ashley Road
  Box Cottage, 16 Fairfield Road
  1 Fairlawn Road
  Picton House
  Rennison's Baths and Terrett's Mills
  69 and 71 Richmond Road
  6 St Andrew's Road
  108 York Road

Unpublished Manuscripts:
Barkshire, Alison Munson, 'Montpelier, the Development of a Bristol Suburb, 1800-1900' in Cheltenham Road Library, Ref. AN 24066117
Harrison, Jo., 'Montpelier, 1750-1900' (a preliminary study for a University of Bristol Extra Mural Class), *c*.1978
Hewitt, F., 'Population and Urban Growth in East Bristol, 1800-1914' (Ph D thesis, University of Bristol,1968)
Sudworth, Bridget, 'Picton Street –Nucleus for a Community' (Enrichment Studies, University of Bristol School of Education, 1980)

Secondary Sources
Alford, B.W.E., 'The Economic Development of Bristol in the Nineteenth Century', in *Essays in Bristol and Gloucestershire History*, P. McGrath and J. Cannon (eds)., Bristol and Gloucestershire Archaeological Society, 1976
Anderson, Charles, *A City and Its Cinemas*, Redcliffe Press, 1983
Atkyns, Richard, *Military Memoirs of the Civil War*, ed. Peter Young
Belsey, James and Reid, Helen, *West at War*, Redcliffe Press, 1990
Bentley, Nicholas, *Selections from the Reminiscences of Captain Grownow – Aide de Camp to General Picton*, Folio Society, 1977

Brown, Horatio, *J.A. Symons, a biography compiled from his correspondence*, London, J.C. Nimmo, 1895

Bush, Graham, *Bristol and Its Municipal Government, 1820-1851*, Bristol Record Society, Vol. XXIX, 1976

Crick, Clare, *Victorian Buildings in Bristol*, Bristol and West Building Society and City Art Gallery, 1975

Dawson, David, 'And Bethel Shall Come To Nought', article in *Avon Past*, Journal of Avon Archaeological Council and Avon Local History Association, Issue 3, Autumn 1980

Dening, C.F.W., *Old Inns of Bristol*, Bristol, J.Wright, 1943

Dunn, Sarah, *Colston Girls' School: The First Hundred Years*, Redcliffe Press, 1991.

Eason, Helena, *Bristol's Historic Inns*, Redcliffe Press, 1982

Evans, John, *A Chronological Outline of the history of Bristol and the Stranger's Guide*, Bristol, the author, 1824

Fanshawe, Bingham, *Horfield Miscellanea*, Portsmouth, the author, 1906

Gomme, Andor, Jenner, Michael and Little, Bryan, *Bristol, An Architectural History*, Lund Humphries, London, 1979

Greenwood, T., *Public Libraries, their organisation, uses and management*, Cassell, London, 3rd edn, 1890

Hamilton, H., *The English Brass and Copper Industries before 1800*, London, Longmans, 1926

Harding, Dermot (ed.), *Bristol Charters 1155-1373*, Vol.1, Bristol Record Society, 1930

Harrison, Jo., 'Early Montpelier, I and II', *Avon Archaeological Newsletter*, Spring and Autumn, 1977

Harvey, C., and Press, J. (eds), *Studies in the Business History of Bristol*, Bristol Academic Press, 1988

Howell, E.B. (ed.), *A Complete Collection of State Trials*, 1817

Hyamson, A.M., *Dictionary of English Phrases*, London, Routledge, 1922

Irving, Laurence, *The Actor and His World*, Faber and Faber, 1951

Ivamy, Hardy E.R. (ed.), *Mozeley and Whiteley's Law Dictionary*, 10th edn., Butterworths, 1988

Lambert, David, *Historic Public Parks, Bristol*, Avon Gardens Trust, 2000

Large, Davis, *The Municipal Government of Bristol, 1851-1901*, Bristol Record Society

Latimer, John, *Annals of Bristol in the Eighteenth Century*, Bristol, 1893; *Annals of Bristol in the Nineteenth Century*, Bristol, 1887; *Annals of Bristol 1887-1900*, Bristol, 1902

Leech, Joseph, *Rural Rides of the Bristol Churchgoer*, edited and published by Alan Sutton, Bristol, 1982

McCann, Graham, *Cary Grant: A Class Apart*, Fourth Estate, 1996

McGrath, Patrick (ed.), *A Bristol Miscellany*, Bristol Record Society, Vol. XXXVII, 1985

Meller, H.E., *Leisure and the Changing City, 1870-1914*, Routledge and Kegan Paul, 1976

Mowl, Timothy, *To Build the Second City*, Redcliffe Press, 1991

Murphy, Graham, *Founders of the National Trust*, Christopher Helm, 1987

Muthesius, Stephan, *The English Terraced House*, Yale University Press, 1982

Nicholls, J.F. and Taylor, John, *Bristol Past and Present*, 3 Vols, Arrowsmith, Bristol, 1881-2

Oakley, Mike, *Bristol Suburban, 1840-1900*, Redcliffe Press, 1990

Ports of the Bristol Channel, The London Printing and Engraving Co., 1893

Priest, G. and Cobb, P. (eds), *The Fight for Bristol*, Bristol Civic Society and Redcliffe Press, 1980

Punter, John, *Design Control in Bristol, 1940-1990*, Redcliffe Press, 1990

Reid, Helen, *Bristol Blitz, The Untold Story*, Redcliffe Press, 1998

Salmon, Arthur, *A Book of English Places*, Ernest Benn, London, 1934

Salvation Army, *A Century of Blood and Fire, 1880-1980*, Centenary Publication, 1980

Seyer, Samuel, *Memoirs Historical and Topographical of Bristol and its Neighbourhood*, Bristol, J.M. Gutch, Vol. 1 (1821), Vol. II (1823)

Smith, A.H., *The Place Names of Gloucestershire*, English Place-Name Society, Vol.XL, Part 3, The Lower Severn Valley and The Forest of Dean, Cambridge University Press, 1964

Sprigg, Joshua, *Anglia Rediviva*

Stone, G.F., *Bristol: As It Was And As It Is* (reprinted, with additions, from the *Bristol Evening News*, 1908-9), Bristol, W. Reid, 1909

Vincent, Mike, *Lines to Avonmouth*, Oxford Publishing Company, 1979

Wigan, Eve, *A Tale of Gordano: A History of the Gordano Region of Somerset*, Taunton, Wessex Press, 1950

Local History Pamphlets, published by the Bristol Branch of the Historical Association:

Cobb, Peter G., *The Oxford Movement in Nineteenth Century Bristol* (no. 68), 1988

Gibson, Cyril, *The Bristol School Board, 1871-1903* (no. 93), 1997

Lamb, Peter G., *Electricity in Bristol, 1863-1948* (no. 48), 1981

Nabb, Harold, *The Bristol Gas Industry, 1815-1949* (no. 67), 1987

Nabb, Harold, *The Bristol Gas Light Company: The Breillat Dynasty of Engineers* (no. 83), 1993

Ralph, E. and Cobb, P., *New Anglican Churches in Nineteenth Century Bristol* (no. 76), 1991

Index

Plan of Bristol by B. Donne, 1826.